Joseph Booth

Africa for the African

Edited by Laura Perry

A Kachere Text

C L A I M

Die Deutsche Bibliothek - CIP - Einheitsaufnahme

Booth, Joseph:
Africa for the African / Joseph Booth. -
Ed. by Laura Perry,
CLAIM, Christian Literature Association in Malawi, Blantyre. -
Nachdr. der Ausg. 1897.
Bonn: Verl. für Kultur und Wiss., 1996
(Kachere text ; No. 6)
ISBN 3-926105-68-2
NE: GT

Copyright 1996

All rights reserved. No part of this publication may be reproduced, stored in a retrieval system, or transmitted in any form or by any means, electronic, mechanical, photocopying, recording or otherwise, without prior permission from the publishers.

Published by the
Christian Literature Association in Malawi (CLAIM),
P.O. Box 503, Blantyre, Malawi
ISBN 99908-16-03-4

ISSN 1025-0956

Copublished in Europe by
Verlag für Kultur und Wissenschaft
(Culture and Science Publ.)
Dr. Thomas Schirrmacher,
Friedrichstr. 38, D-53111 Bonn, Germany

Printed 1998 in Malawi by Assemblies of God Press, P.O. Box 5749, Limbe

Joseph Booth

Africa for the African

Edited by Laura Perry

Kachere Text No. 6

CLAIM
Christian Literature Association in Malawi
Blantyre
Culture and Science Publ., Bonn
1996

Kachere Series,
P.O. Box 1037, Zomba, Malawi

This book is part of the Kachere Series, a range of books on religion and theology in Malawi. Books published so far are:

Kachere Books:

Matembo S. Nzunda, Kenneth R. Ross (eds), *Church, Law and Political Transition in Malawi 1992-1994.*
Kenneth R. Ross, *Gospel Ferment in Malawi: Theological Essays.*
Kenneth R. Ross (ed.), *Christianity in Malawi: A Source Book.*

Kachere Monographs:

Andrew C. Ross, *Blantyre Mission and the Making of Modern Malawi.*
Harry Langworthy, *"Africa for the African": The Life of Joseph Booth.*
K.R. Ross (ed.), *God, People and Power in Malawi.*
Isabel A. Phiri, *Women, Presbyterianism and Patriarchy.*
M. Schoffeleers, *Religion and the Dramatisation of Life.*

Kachere Texts:

K.R. Ross (ed.), *Church, University and Theological Education in Malawi.*
Silas S. Ncozana, *Sangaya: A Leader in the Synod of Blantyre CCAP.*
Peggy Owens (ed.), *When Maize and Tobacco are not Enough.*
Stephen Kauta Msiska, *Golden Buttons.*
Hubert Reijnaerts, Ann Nielsen, M. Schoffeleers, *Montfortians in Malawi.*

The Kachere Series is the publications arm of the Department of Theology and Religious Studies of the University of Malawi.

Series Editors: J.C. Chakanza, F.L. Chingota, Klaus Fiedler, H. Mijoga, Fulata Moyo, Martin Ott, Isabel A. Phiri, K.R. Ross, J. Tengatenga

Editor's Preface

Joseph Booth's *Africa for the African* was first published one hundred years ago, in 1897. Months later a second edition followed, also dated in 1897. The ideas presented by Booth were radical for the time period, and as history tells us, his prescription was neither widely accepted nor followed in his lifetime or after it. Yet Booth's commitment to the development of Africa for the benefit of its people remains an example to modern readers.

Joseph Booth (1851 -1932) was a visionary and devoted Christian. In the ten years that he served as a missionary to Nyasaland, now Malawi, he helped to establish eight missions through seven different denominations. Though Booth changed denominational affiliation readily, he never compromised his belief in the ability and the rights of the African people.

At the time of the writing in the late nineteenth century, increasing nationalism, industrialization and mercantilism in Europe was resulting in the worldwide expansion of European empires. Just thirteen years earlier, in an effort to expand their spheres of influence into Africa, European leaders had met in Berlin in 1884-5 to carve up the continent. But as Cecil Rhodes, King Leopold and other Europeans were in the midst of building personal and political empires in Africa, a few unconventional missionaries like Booth struggled with what the gospel had to say about their presence in Africa. While many missionaries either actively encouraged or passively watched the expansion of colonial authority, Booth criticized the colonial regimes. Because Booth saw clear social and political implications in the gospel message, he spoke out against the mistreatment of Africans on European estates and the need for representation of the Africans' desires in the government of their land.

On the centenary of the publication of *Africa for the African*, Africa has not yet achieved the full independence Booth envisioned. It was sixty years after the publication of Booth's treatise that the first African colony gained its political independence. Yet to this day much of Africa has not achieved economic independence due to massive international debt and industries remaining in the hands of large multinational corporations and a small African elite. The Kachere Series is therefore pleased to enable Booth to "speak out" again to remind us that there is much work still to be done to reach the goal of "Africa for the African".

What follows is a reproduction of the second edition of Booth's book. The editor has taken the prerogative to correct spelling errors which appeared in either edition without noting these, unless a change in a letter resulted in a different word. Booth's alternation between American and British spelling has been maintained. All other changes in the second edition, which diverged from the original text of the first edition, have been footnoted. It is not known whether these changes resulted from new ideas and insights Booth may have had following the first edition, or if they were simply corrections of omissions and incorrectly typed words in the first edition. Booth's biographer, Harry Langworthy, suggests that many of these changes could in fact be due to corrections in wording resulting from the typist's inability to decipher Booth's poor handwriting. Aside from the annotations inserted by the editor, the only addition to Booth's work is the index.

Booth's formatting has been maintained as much as possible, i.e. using italics, bold and capitalization only where Booth himself did for emphasis. However, books and newspapers have been italicized per modern usage and extended quotes have been set off to ease the reading. Because the pagination which follows differs from the second edition, the original page numbers are noted in brackets. Where a page break occurred in the middle of a word, the new page is noted immediately following the word.

The book can be divided roughly into three sections. The first and primary section presents Booth's analysis of the colonial situation and the status of Africans therein as the problem to be addressed. He continues then, with a plan to resolve the situation through such programs as African-American repatriation, African-run industrial missions, and perhaps most importantly, political independence for the African. In the second section, entitled "The Author's Apology", Booth adds a personal touch by including a short autobiography, which details his call to mission work and presents his reasoning behind writing the book. The final section is comprised of schedules which include a blueprint for the proposed African Christian Union and numerous figures to support Booth's earlier claims of economic feasibility of the plans presented in the first portion of the book.

One of the great improvements to the second edition was the inclusion of six new pages of photographs and explanatory material which were inserted throughout the book without renumbering the pages. Because the pagination in the current edition differs from the second edition and the photographs do not necessarily relate to the text in the body of the book, these pages have been reproduced at the end of this volume, following the schedules.

I wish to extend sincere thanks to the late Harry Langworthy for making copies of the two editions available to the Kachere Series and to Don Sanford of the Seventh Day Baptist Historical Society for providing copies of the photographs. I am also grateful to the Kachere editors for the opportunity to work on this book, with special appreciation to Klaus Fiedler for his support in this endeavor.

Laura Perry
Washington, DC, November 1997

AFRICA

-FOR THE-

AFRICAN.

DEDICATED

First, to VICTORIA, QUEEN OF GREAT BRITAIN.

Second, to the BRITISH and AMERICAN CHRISTIAN

People.

Third and Specially to the AFRO-AMERICAN people of the

United States of America

-BY-

JOSEPH BOOTH, MISSIONARY,
NYASSALAND,
EAST CENTRAL AFRICA.

AFRICA FOR THE AFRICAN.

———*———

The author's apology for the contents of this pamphlet will be found in its closing pages.

The motto, "Africa for the African," is not new; and at first sight it seems strange that such a standard should need to be raised. "Europe for the Europeans" would seem an absurd phrase to formulate, since the Europeans would not tolerate the thought that any other race would be found audacious enough, powerful enough, or even unscrupulous enough to dispossess them.

Although Africa is as large as Europe and North America combined, yet her vast territory, it is assumed, belongs no more to the African race. Any rights they had to administer or develop their country are taken as terminated and beyond consideration. The words heading this pamphlet are used, therefore, as a brief standard of protest against any and every person or persons, be they obscure or prominent, whether individuals or nations in combination, who ruthlessly assert their purpose, power, or right to take from the African race the African's land.

The numerical strength of the African race is admitted to be about one-seventh of the population of the whole earth. The vastness and wealth of his God-given country is in keeping with his numerical importance. His physical powers and mental capacity are probably equal to those of any branch of the human family.

Why then has he not taken and maintained a befitting place amongst the great races of the earth? Because the day of Africa has yet to come.

During the past three centuries the African's progress has doubtless been greatly retarded by the ungenerous and often criminal treatment he has been awarded by his European neighbors. As these latter emerged from barbarism and entered upon a period of commercial and territorial enterprise, discovering and seizing upon new countries,

AFRICA FOR THE AFRICAN.

subduing and often destroying their inhabitants, they ruthlessly set to work to people some of these countries with slaves plundered from the coasts of Africa, and thus inaugurated one of the most, if not absolutely the most gigantic and long sustained crimes of modern times. To supply this accursed demand for slave labor, the coastal African tribes were primed to prey upon the tribes of the interior, [4] and thus the hands of the Africans were kept constantly imbrued in each other's blood.

The British, Portuguese, Dutch and Spanish were the most prominent in this nefarious traffic in human flesh. The proposal of the European was thus to appropriate the person and labor of the African.

So enormous and long-sustained a wrong, though clung to with almost fiendish tenacity by the interested class, was doomed to be abandoned before the growing power of unfettered Christian teaching, and this colossal injustice received its final death blow by means of the great American civil war, which forever burst asunder the fetters of the Negro slave.

But the unhallowed spirit of European greed for aggrandizement at the African's expense was not, though sorely wounded, to die so speedy a death. The flagrant and revolting nature of the old method must per force be abandoned: but the resolve to exploit the African in some form yet remained.

As the wonderful resources of his country became known, and the treasures of precious stones, gold and agricultural products were revealed, the desire to posses the property of the African, rather than his person, became manifest. The European scramble for the African's land then began in earnest. The purpose of certain European powers to appropriate large sections of African territory, was, however, cleverly glossed over, more or less, with a philanthropic film.

The slave raiding, which at one time these same powers had industriously fostered and which the Arab still prosecuted, was now to be

AFRICA FOR THE AFRICAN.

extirpated by the wholesale appropriation of territory and the subduing of the inhabitants.

The partition, or plunder, of Africa by this concerted agreement, or conspiracy, of certain European powers, was conveniently arranged, and the closing decade of the nineteenth century witnesses the SECOND MAGNIFICENTLY UNSCRUPULOUS proposal of the European[1] to harness and exploit his African neighbor. The former clumsy proposal to annex and transplant the African's person was costly, cumbersome and infamous; the present proposal to purloin the land under his feet and adroitly to utilize the African as an instrument to disclose, develop and deposit its resources for the European's benefit, is the self-same in spirit, but more ingeniously dressed, further reaching in its effects, and far less likely to be challenged.

It is a proposal to deprive 200 million of people of their birthright; to seize upon their property and permanently drain the wealth of Africa and the African's labor into European channels.

The proposal reminds one of the comment of the American judge, Chief Justice Taney,[2] relating to a certain class in the Southern American states:

> They did not consider that the black man had *any rights* which white men were bound to respect.[3]

---

[1] 1st ed has "Europeans" in place of "the European".

[2] Roger Brooke Taney (1777-1864) was the fifth chief justice of the US Supreme Court, a position to which he was appointed by President Andrew Jackson in 1835. He is remembered especially for the majority opinion he authored in the Dred Scott case in 1857. For more on Taney, see Carl B. Swisher's biography of the judge, Roger B. Taney, (New York: Macmillan Company, 1935).

[3] This controversial statement was part of Taney's opinion issued in Dred Scott vs. John A. Sanford in which the African-American Dred Scott

AFRICA FOR THE AFRICAN.

[5] As in the days of man-stealing, Britain was to the front, so in the modern process of land-snatching, Britain is again distinguished by her prominence.

To the unprejudiced observer and to the educated African, she is a marvel of inconsistency, if not criminality, since by her national religion, she gratuitously and systematically asserts her belief in the commands:

> "Thou shalt not covet;
> Thou shalt not steal;
> Thou shalt not kill;"

---

sued his owner to obtain his freedom from slavery. Scott began his suit in 1846 in the state of Missouri where legal precedence had repeatedly granted freedom to slaves who had resided in free territories before entering or, as in Scott's case, returning to states in which slavery was legal. In the appeal to the US Supreme Court, Taney concluded that because Scott was a Negro and a slave in the state of Missouri, he was not a citizen of the United States and therefore could not bring suit against Sanford.

Booth was among many who misrepresented Taney's statement: "they had no rights". Booth suggests that Taney was citing the opinion of Southern American slave-holders. In fact Taney's argument was that this opinion had been widely held by the entire white population at the time that the US was founded, so, Taney concluded, blacks could not be considered citizens of the country. Taney explained that at the writing of the US Constitution:

> They [blacks] had for more than a century before been regarded as beings of an inferior order, and altogether unfit to associate with the white race, either in social or political relations; and so far inferior, that they had no rights which the white man was bound to respect; and that the negro might justly and lawfully be reduced to slavery for his benefit.... This opinion was at the time fixed and universal in the civilized portion of the white race.

See Don Fehrenbacher *The Dred Scott Case: Its Significance in American Law and Politics*, (New York: Oxford University Press, 1978), 347. Although many Southerners applauded Taney's conclusion, the court's decision was widely criticized by abolitionists and was one of the catalysts for the US Civil War.

AFRICA FOR THE AFRICAN.

yet, most effectually, deliberately and continuously she does all three of these in pursuit of her ruthless African annexation policy.

Her various Christian churches send forth into Africa in good faith, their messengers of "peace on earth and good will toward men;"[4] yet these often prove to be but the forerunner of another set of men, sent to appropriate, to kill, to tax and subjugate. Our words are of peace, but our acts are of war.

No sooner has the missionary led his convert into the freedom and light of God's word than he discerns these things and discovers we are proclaiming that which condemns ourselves and exposes the wrongs we perpetrate so shamelessly.

He naturally asks why, if the missionaries be truly men of God, and not in concert with the wrong-doers, do they not solemnly and sternly denounce the authors of the evil? Are they the victims of the fear of man which "bringeth a snare?"

The African's Heritage.

It is doubtful whether any race has a grander natural heritage than has the African race. Its full value is not yet known, but enough is known to create a widespread feeling of envy in other peoples. In gold and precious stones, Africa is doubtless the richest continent on the globe. But its greatest wealth lies in its undeveloped power to produce and furnish to the world cotton, Indian corn, coffee, cocoa, tea, sugar, and indeed, all tropical and subtropical articles of commerce.

The African native as well as his relative, the Negro of America, is gradually, though slowly, awakening to recognize this. When these

---

[4] See Luke 2:14.

AFRICA FOR THE AFRICAN.

enter heartily into possession of, and utilize the resources of their great heritage, and use them to diffuse Christian and industrial knowledge throughout the land, the day of Africa will have come.

[6] No longer will the African be the despised and down-trodden people, exploited at will by all comers, but will be found well able to take and hold his rightful place and enjoy his new-found strength of Christian unity and brotherhood. Then he will rejoice as a strong man in his strength.

How Shall This be Brought About?

To one who knows the raw African, not as he is represented by despisers and haters of his race, but as he really is when approached and treated with moderate kindness, the problem does not seem difficult; nor does the time seem distant when these things shall be accomplished.

The untutored African, taken as a whole, is as promising and encouraging a material to work upon as his country is full of promise to the wealth-seeker.

HE IS NOT A LAZY MAN, though it is one of the commonest assertions of his maligners that he is lazy; indeed, this is the favorite South African excuse for ill-treating him. The writer has had to work with hundreds of Central Africans for months at a time, and can testify from experience that if once the native clearly understands what is required of him, and he has agreed to do it, and if he be treated as a man and not as a dog or brute, the African will work long, hard and cheerfully in a way that no other race would or could work in a similar climate. The popular method in South Africa is first to denounce and then to drive him.

AFRICA FOR THE AFRICAN.

HE IS NOT A DISHONEST MAN. To this day it is a standing puzzle to the writer how the Central African comes to be so honest. You may trust him with hundreds of loads of goods which he knows the value of and wants. You may let him go out of sight for days together; yet he will turn up at the end of the journey with everything marvelously safe. He is a marvel of endurance and seems content to give the maximum labor for the minimum payment. Certain it is, that in no part of the European world could an equal number of poor laboring men, called hastily together as these are, be found, who would per hundred, bear the same amount of temptation and come through as clear-handed.

HE IS NOT A STUPID MAN. Perhaps no one thing more astonishes the European than to discover how quickly the uncontaminated Central African absorbs what he has to teach him, and waits for more. No industry is taught him but he is soon the master of it. In acquiring a new language he learns much quicker than the European, though not so systematically.

His powers of imitation are great and will develop; they enable him to quickly adopt such features of European civilization as he may consider worth the having.

[7] His inventive faculties are not so apparent, though judging by the quick-witted answers or questions he produces impromptu, it seems likely he will not be found ultimately wanting in power to originate and devise.

HE IS NOT A QUARRELSOME MAN. The discovery of this comes as a great surprise to the man who has gathered from the books of travelers the impression that the African is always ready to fight and quarrel. This is not so. The contrary is the case, for he is, as a rule, a very decided lover of peace, and will gravitate to that rule, or those conditions which will secure to him the greatest promise of peace. In this matter, there is, however, some difference, some tribes are so much lovers of peace that they will make for peace at any price, others will only make peace on conditions which satisfy them. Nevertheless, the

AFRICA FOR THE AFRICAN.

African people as a whole are used to obey and like to be ruled by a strong power or chief, even if somewhat tyrannical. The individuals or tribes who really like war are very few, indeed. At the same time, it is true that inter-tribal warfare has in the past been their chronic curse, not by choice; it has been forced upon them by centuries of demand for slaves by European and Arabian slave merchants.

More competent judges than the writer hold the same convictions as to the capacity, trustworthiness, tractableness and general ability of the Central African tribes, notably the Ajawa, Manganja, Chickunda, Makalolo, Angoni, Atonga, Chipeta and N'Konde.[5]

The following extracts relating to these from the last report of Her Majesty's Consul-General, Sir H.H. Johnston[6], to the British Parliament show that he has been impressed with the same features, and looks upon them as the groundwork upon which to develop an important revenue for the British government. He writes of B.C. Africa:[7]

> The present number of European planters is about 100. Beside these European Planters it is pleasant to be able to record that six natives who have risen, most of them, from the position of scholars in the mission schools, have started and are doing well as coffee planters. One of these men is a native chief ... who has gone in vigorously for coffee planting.
>
> It only needs a sufficiency of native labor to make this country relatively healthy and amazingly rich.
>
> I entertain great hopes of the intellectual development of the Negro of Central Africa. I do not know whether he comes of a more intelligent stock than those west coast tribes that have

---

[5] These ethnic groups are now known as the Yao, Mang'anja, Chikunda, Makololo, Ngoni, Tonga, Chipeta and Nkonde respectively.
[6] Booth has "Johnson" instead of "Johnston" throughout both editions.
[7] British Central Africa.

AFRICA FOR THE AFRICAN.

furnished the type found in many of the old American slaves from which the ordinary idea of the Negro is derived, but certainly it is encouraging to notice the rapid way in which our Central African natives are learning what the white man can teach them. We have here at Zomba one European head-printer at the government press. All the other printers [8] are natives who have been locally trained ... and who from untutored young savages of two, four, six or twelve months ago have now become skilled printers, having at the same time mastered a considerable knowledge of English and of reading and writing.

They are equally keen and apt in their military drill, in acquiring a knowledge of brickmaking, masonry work, carpentering and even of clerical work and accounts.

Our mission here is undoubtlessly to raise the Negro of Central Africa into a civilized nationality, for we can never hope to colonize the bulk of this country with the white race. What we seek to aim at is the education of the black people into a State dependent on the British Empire in matters of general policy, and thrown open unrestrictedly to British trade and enterprise. The people, therefore, must work out their own salvation with such help we can give them as masters and teachers. - *Blue Book, Africa, No 5. 1896. Price, 9d. Eyer & Spottiswood, East Harding St., Fleet St., London, E. C.*

As a palpable proof of the peaceable disposition of the tribes within the protectorate in Central Africa, it may be mentioned that the same report records the fact that although the country has only been attached by the British for a period of five years, and has only an European population of 289 persons, male and female; yet this smaller number, 100 of whom are planters and 70 to 80 are missionaries, suffices to control, tax and appropriate the land of 844,420 natives without any considerable protest on their part; the proportion being about 3,000 natives to each European. The writer has often questioned these natives as to why they so readily give up their land and liberty to an alien race;

AFRICA FOR THE AFRICAN.

the answer invariably being, "We have no other way to get calico to clothe our bodies, or to get the knowledge the white man brings."

Outside the somewhat small piece of country called the British Protectorate, there lie vast blocks of fertile country comprising a thousand millions of acres which are mapped off on the present-day maps, to be entered into and appropriated at leisure by Portugal, Belgium, Germany and the South African Company.

In this vast tract of country, where the people know practically nothing of the overbearing proposals of these countries, the present European population is not more than one to each seven or ten thousand natives. To save these from the iron heel of the land monopolist, these need knowledge; who will give it them?

The outrageous nature of the concerted proposal to claim these vast tracts and to convert the resident native into a tax-payer in order to furnish the means for his further subjugation, is as apparent as it is unscrupulous.

How then shall "Africa for the African" become an accomplished fact?

[9] There are three ways visible. The first, the simplest and noblest, is for the various European powers who have planned the "partition" of Africa to ACT HONESTLY and give to the African the same rights they would insist upon themselves. Let them abandon the process of stealthy absorption of the African's property and do him common justice. Let them simply administer his country in his interest and with economy, bestowing all surplus revenue upon his uplifting and development. Is common honesty and kindly aid too much to expect from enlightened Christian powers, professing adherence to the word of God?

It cannot surely be that our high-minded Christian statesmen of the nineteenth century can be intentionally guilty of the cowardly barbarism of claiming the resources of a great, yet poor people, simply be-

AFRICA FOR THE AFRICAN.

cause they are defenseless and ignorant! It seems beyond credence that our leaders should possess nobility only in name; that the first and final note in their treatment of their African neighbour should be that of substituting "might" for "right" as in the barbarous days of old.

If this BE NOT SO, let it be made manifest by some public record that they simply enter and hold their respective sections of Africa IN TRUST during the period of their African brother's minority, placing a period to their self-assumed trust.[8]

As one English-born subject of Her Majesty, the Queen Victoria, to whom the present usurpation policy in Africa is odious and obnoxious in an extreme degree, the writer hopes and prays that Her Majesty personally, and her advisers collectively, will reconsider the present and prospective attitude toward the native Africans generally, and in particular those dwelling in the vast tracts of territory recently annexed and known respectively as:

(1) The British Central African Protectorate.
(2) British Imperial East Africa.
(3) The British South African Company's Territory.
(4) The Royal Niger Company's Territory and Niger Coast Protectorate;

over the latter two of which Britain holds the ultimate jurisdiction by reason of her reserve power under the charters granted.

Seeing that the British South African Chartered Company claim to be the owners of some 750,000 square miles, more or less, and the Royal

---

[8] Soon after writing these words, Booth, in the Petition to Queen Victoria, set a time limit of 21 years. The Petition was published in the *Central African Times* on July 22, 1899. It has been reprinted in *Christianity in Malawi: A Sourcebook*, edited by Kenneth R. Ross, (Gweru: Mambo Press, 1996). For the administration's reaction to the Petition and Booth's subsequent exile see Harry Langworthy, *"Africa for the African": The Life of Joseph Booth*, (Blantyre: CLAIM, 1996), 121-131.

AFRICA FOR THE AFRICAN.

Niger Company assert their rights over a territory of some 500,000 square miles of West African territory by virtue of 235 treaties with pagan, and some 170 treaties or more with Mohammedan chiefs, it is submitted that the welfare of the multitude of Africans dwelling in such vast areas should be under Imperial oversight and control, and freed from the administration of companies whose sole business is the production of wealth.

Without entertaining the fear of, or courting the favour of any person or persons, and as one individual accountable to Almighty God for the resolute, [10] and believing employment of one person's influence to withstand unrighteousness and oppression, whether on the part of individuals or nations combined, the writer has no alternative but to urge upon the British executive leaders the patient reconsideration of the compact into which she has entered with certain European powers for the partition, invasion, conquest and exploitation of Africa; the putative cause of action being the suppression of traffic in slaves. Most strenuously is it urged on behalf of these territories where British colonists' interests do not as yet merit the consideration awarded them in the older possessions of the South, that Britain, while she has the opportunity, leads the way in an amended policy, definitely pledged to hand back to the Africans themselves at some not distant period, the whole of these possessions; in the meantime, governing, developing and taxing primarily in the interest of, and for the present and future uplifting and enlightening of the Negro race.

Britain can well afford to be not only just but generous. Let her go a step further in setting an example of a clean-handed, full-measured policy to the long enyoked Negro.

Let Britain, in a spirit of restitution for past, but unredeemed wrongs, use her present day of opportunity to restore or facilitate the restoration of the scattered Negro people of the West India Islands and America to their fatherland; and if she can not go the length of a money grant per family, then let a freehold grant of a block of land be

AFRICA FOR THE AFRICAN.

selected by each Negro adult or head of a family prepared to return either with his own means or means otherwise provided. The sections of country referred to would readily support, in addition to the present native population, the whole body of expatriated Negroes, even though their number were fivefold the present ten millions.

Without any real cost to herself, Britain can confer upon the African race, by the restoration of the land to the people, and by free gifts of land to the returning Negro, a greater real benefit than by the act of emancipation, which cost her twenty millions sterling, since that effected about one million of persons only, but left them destitute.

Will Britain be thus magnanimous? and thus make
"AFRICA FOR THE AFRICANS"
something more than a hope?

Why should not the memorable reign of our good Queen, Victoria, be crowned with one more imperishable act calculated to breathe a new inspiration into a long despised and cruelly treated race?

The writer is convinced that could our noblest leaders bring themselves to a personal and candid consideration of the Africans' present-day stripped and helpless condition as the outcome of the comparatively recent anti-slave-trading-concerted-crusade, they would refuse to be guilty of a territorial usurpation policy, dressed in the garb of philanthropy. For nations to [11] combine to exterminate Arab slave-trading, was good, but to perpetuate the combination in order to possess the African and his country "en masse" is surely an enormous wrong.

That the motives of such organizations as the Anti-Slavery Society and the Aborigines' Protection Society are absolutely pure of any selfish purpose, is beyond doubt, and therefore, to them also is this appeal directed to take a yet further step and quit themselves of all complicity in the present day of enormity of a surreptitious, yet forceful, appro-

AFRICA FOR THE AFRICAN.

priation of all that the African holds dear: viz., his land, his home and his liberty.

The vastly more humane policy pursued and native confidence enjoyed by such an administrator as the one who has in a brief period and in an economical manner evolved the present order out of comparative chaos in the country now known as The British Central African Protectorate, as compared with the South African Chartered Company, has been highly gratifying to observers on the spot who hold that "right" comes before "might."

Probably in no part of recently occupied Africa is there extended to the native an equal opportunity to elevate himself and obtain recognition according to his merit. The vulgar, common and stupid prejudice as to the color of persons' skins is but faintly felt by the natives of B.C. Africa as contrasted with those of the South, who receive, as a rule, much coarser treatment.

Notwithstanding the genuine good will displayed by Sir H.H. Johnston and his almost enthusiastic confidence in the capacity and malleableness of the Central African, there gleams through the mellifluous report of this versatile administrator, the old and sinister purpose of aggrandizement on the part of Britain by means of the skillfully adjusted pressure of the weak and ignorant African.

Whilst in South Africa the European is sufficiently in force to extract a 14s. hut tax from even the warlike Zulu for the privilege of being permitted to exist on the land he formerly owned; under the considerate Consul-General of B.C. Africa, the present demand upon the natives does not exceed 3s. yearly per hut. The manner in which the vision of future wealth for the European is to be realized is defined with refreshing politeness. (See Blue Book, Africa, No. 5. 1896.)

> The native labor question is almost the most important question which can now claim the attention of those administering the

AFRICA FOR THE AFRICAN.

> protectorate.... It only needs a sufficiency of native labor to make this country relatively healthy and amazingly rich.
>
> A "gentle insistence" that the native should contribute his fair share to the revenue of the country by paying his tax, is all that is necessary on our part to his taking that share in life's labour which no human being should evade. At the same time, the Administration is bound to see that [12] the native is fairly treated and that attention is given to his food and general welfare on the part of his European employer.

By all means, let the "gentle insistence" be thus brought to bear, providing there be a distinct renunciation of selfish ends on the part of Britain, the strong. One would fain be able to say, "Britain, the Protector."

Pending or failing this, let us consider the second method of securing "Africa for the African."

As "righteousness exalteth a nation,"[9] so does righteousness exalt the individual in God's sight. If we cannot persuade the rulers of, or the heterogeneous mass of thinkers which composes a nation to act righteously even generously; as individuals we can stand out separately and touch not the unclean thing of national plunder and oppression.

But the religious world will exclaim, "We have nothing to do with politics." This also must be combatted. It is one of the favorite excuses for leaving wickedness in high places to go on unchecked, unchallenged and unremedied. It is a clever evasion born of the craft and subtlety of the devil, from which, "Good Lord, deliver us."

All power, all rightful, all final authority is given to Christ, and his servants are his friends in proportion as they do whatsoever he has commanded. He commands that our neighbor, who has fallen among thieves who have beat him, and stripped him, and left him helpless by the wayside; that his servants shall "go and do likewise" to the

---

[9] Proverbs 14:34.

AFRICA FOR THE AFRICAN.

Samaritan.[10] The measure He bids us give is good measure pressed down, shaken together and running over.[11] The "pass-by-on-the-other-side" servants do not come far short in heartlessness and guilt to the spoilers themselves.

Let those Christians who are touched with compassion for the African form themselves into a Christian Union, solemnly pledged to do all that the power of God will enable them to do, and give to Africa's sons and daughters their full rights under the gospel of peace and good will, both in word and deed.

Hitherto, our missionary operations have, in the main, been content to preach and declare the good tidings; but Christ's Gospel is one of acts as well as of words. It demands that we shall do and not speak and hear only. Its requirements are simple, searching and definite.

> Therefore, all things whatsoever ye would that men should do to you, do ye even so to them.[12]

We must enlarge our missionary methods somewhat if we would do for Africa as we would wish done for ourselves if placed in like circumstances. We should wish for the Gospel of good will relating to the present life as well as the life to come. We should wish for a brotherly hand to guide and uplift, not to exploit us; we should wish for knowledge how to develop the resources of our land, but not for the enrichment of an already rich and [13] foreign power; we should wish to be taught industries, commercial and mining knowledge combined with that of the navigation of our rivers and lakes as well as the ocean

---

[10] The parable of the good Samaritan is found in Luke 10:25-37.
[11] See Luke 6:38. The Authorized Version reads: "Give and it shall be given unto you; good measure, pressed down, and shaken together, and running over, shall men give into your bosom. For with the same measure that ye mete withal it shall be measured to you again."
[12] See Matthew 7:12; the verse continues: for this is the law and the prophets.

AFRICA FOR THE AFRICAN.

skirting our shores: but most of all, we should desire to remain free men, and in the possession of the land of our fathers.

It is within the spirit and compass of the Gospel of Jesus Christ, the Son of the living God, to freely impart these things.

As a beginning, therefore, the writer urges the formation of an

AFRICAN CHRISTIAN UNION

by such Christians who wish to be free from passive complicity in the spoliation of the African, but who, on the contrary, wish to impart along with Gospel education, industries, commercial and other needed knowledge.

Such a union is now in process, several persons having solemnly covenanted to place their lives and resources jointly or severally at the disposal of the work. The texts of the objects of this modest effort will be found appended in Schedule A.

In this society there are two classes of members:

1st - Those pledged for life to devote their substance and life effort to the work, and

2nd - Those who are subscribers only.

The covenant entered into by the first named class is as follows:

We the undersigned do hereby solemnly vow before God and men to devote our lives and substance to the uplifting of the African race as follows:

1st - By the spread of the Gospel of Jesus Christ throughout the continent of Africa.
2nd - By the restoration of the land of Africa to the African people.
3rd - By the restoration of the Negroes to the fatherland from which they were stolen, i. e., of such as desire to return.

AFRICA FOR THE AFRICAN.

The ordinary subscriber simply engages to contribute in some degree to the funds[13] of the Union, and use his or her influence to forward its objects.

The writer would earnestly entreat every European or American Christian into whose hands this appeal may come, to take a part in this work of making amends, as far may be, to the Negro and African for the wrongs they have sustained in the past and are sustaining in the present at European hands.

Consider what a great and many sided charge this great cloud of African witnesses[14] will have against us as a people in the day of judgement, and let us see to it individually, that our hands are clear of direct or indirect wrongdoing.

Remember that British records testify that at the height of the slave-stealing period, British ships, sanctioned and protected by British laws, [14] conveyed over 100 thousand, yearly, of purchased or purloined slaves from the coast of Africa to British Colonies.

Remember that the Negro has never yet had made to him an offer of being freely returned in a decent manner to the country whence he was taken.

Remember that the labour of over two centuries of slave-toil and abuse has not been requited and that it is an hereditary debt lying upon this generation.

Remember that to merely set free the slave and leave him to group[15] and plod his way through the maze of ostracism and competition to gain his rightful position amongst men is not enough; that until a righteous attempt has been made to make adequate restitution, as far as

---

[13] 1st ed has "fund" here.
[14] See Hebrews 12:1.
[15] It appears that an error was introduced here; the 1st ed has "grope".

AFRICA FOR THE AFRICAN.

may be commensurate with the ability of the British and American People, God will not hold us guiltless.

Remember that in the present day the home of the African race is fast being taken away by European force of arms, and the African is fast being left a great race without a country.

Remember that to be conscious of these enormous wrongs and not to seek to remedy them is to become a passive participator in the guilt, since God has declared:

> If thou sayest, Behold, we knew it not, does not He that pondereth the heart consider it? and He that keepeth thy soul, doth not He know it? and shall not He render to every man according to his works?[16]

Wherefore, let every one who cares to be pure and cleansed from the stain of African guilt stand out separate and solemnly resolve to become one in this generation to make restitution according to their individual ability. To this end the reader is invited to give a largehearted and patient consideration to the objects and methods of the African Christian Union as before referred to. [See Schedule A.]

It is not, perhaps, too much to hope for that one per cent at least of the British and American public will, - providing an adequate propaganda be established to compass the work, - be found willing to freely give an average of one penny (two cents) per day over a ten years period to rectify Negro and African wrongs.

It is not improbable that there will be some noble men and women forthcoming who will be pleased to give substantial sums, perchance their "all" to Christ's African poor and the evangelization of their great country. The Europeans of America number seventy millions, the British people forty millions, assuming then, that one per cent of these

---

[16] See Proverbs 24:12.

AFRICA FOR THE AFRICAN.

averaged two cents per day for the period named as a gift, a yearly gross revenue of one and a half million pounds or seven and a half million dollars, would be available: over a ten year's period a gross sum of seventy-five [15] million dollars, or fifteen million pounds, is a not improbable result if the claims of the African race be duly advocated and understood.

Let this sum be cautiously expended, not on charity, but on reproductive efforts: viz., one-half upon reproductive, self-supporting mission effort, the remaining half upon Negro Christian settlements, composed of Negro families who have chosen to return to Africa. Both sections of work to be, as far as possible, conducted by Negro agents or African native Christians.

Such a capital sum being once available and studiously concentrated upon reproductive and self-propagating methods of working, is not unlikely to prove sufficient to solve at one time, two great problems, viz:

(1) The evangelization of Africa, and
(2) The so-called "American Negro problem,"

issuing jointly, may we not hope in the accomplishment of restoring

AFRICA TO THE AFRICAN,

the people to whom the hand of God first gave it?

At this point the reader will doubtless say: "show more fully how this may reasonably be hoped for." In response, the writer, having had some years experience in the designing, founding and subsequent working out of Industrial missions[17] of the kind suggested, [see

---

[17] Booth described his views on industrial missions in "The Greatest Work in the World - A Plea for Missionary Enterprise", which appeared in *Missionary Review of the World* (1892). Booth felt that industrial missions could solve the problem of overtaxed mission budgets as well as leading the African church closer to independence. See Langworthy, *The Life of Joseph Booth*, 25-8.

apology at the close] ventures to ask for a patient hearing, notwithstanding the fact that such methods are not as yet favored by most missionary organizations.

That the possibilities likely to accrue from each line of working are large, will be gathered from the following: take first the Industrial mission basis; experience has shown that £2,000, or thereabouts, is required to equip in East Central Africa, an Industrial station with a full complement of agents and necessary appliances, bringing the same to the period of self-support and with a surplus power for yearly reduplication. Four years, under average circumstances is ample time to accomplish this. Details as to the working out will be found in schedule B.

From the fourth to the seventh year the income steadily advances, owing to the produce of a larger area being available, until the full surplus income of £4,000 to £5,000 per year be realized. £2,000 of this is required for the establishing of a new station, the definite aim of each station, in turn, being to become not only self-supporting, but self-duplicating after the fourth year.

On this system 1,000 acres of land are selected and bought; one[18] half is gradually brought into plantations as a source of income, employing some hundreds of natives; the remaining half being reserved for mission premises, school, hospital, work-shop and native dwellings. At present there is no manifest difficulty in producing an adequate revenue with which to carry [16] out the process of reduplication; it is simply a matter of modest and business-like effort. This is the verdict of some fifty workers who have experience in this form of African mission work.

Recourse to figures will show that a steady progression for a period of twenty-one years gives an arithmetical result of a possible 345 such

---

[18] 1st ed has "and" instead of "one".

centres as the outcome of each parent station. Failures in men and products must doubtless be allowed for, though it may be that the reserve fund created by the surplus income will provide for such contingences. But assuming that fifty per cent of these centres prove financial failures and unable to maintain their rate of progression, the arithmetical result is still so great as to be full of promise. But the half capital assumed as accruing from the penny a day average gift over the period specified should furnish a sufficient sum, if needs be for 646,375 just[19] such centres of Christian teaching, or one to every four hundred inhabitants, reaching a possible 250 million persons. [See schedule C for figures.]

These figures are given in order to show the important degree of promise lying behind Industrial reproductive mission work.

The distinct proposal is that each of these stations should, as far as possible, be worked by Negro or native Christians and freely given over to them in perpetual trust, for the African people, when their competence to control them and maintain their efficiency is fairly assured. Thus the completion of Africa's evangelization would be definitely attempted during the present generation.

Take now the second proposed line of expenditure, the second sum of seven and a half million pounds being assumed to be the measure of the capital available. This may be called

The Negro Christian Settlement Proposal,

which attempts to provide every eligible Negro family desiring to cast in their lot with the African rather than the European race.

---

[19] The word "just" was added in second edition

AFRICA FOR THE AFRICAN.

Strange to say, the[20] contemplation of such proposals in the past has met with a remarkable confluence of opposing opinion flowing from widely separated sources. Here are two: from the heroic Alexander Mackay[21], of Uganda, Central Africa, comes the following just before his death:

> In our teeth is thrown a challenge by an educated African, (Dr Blyden) ... "Africa for the African" and its regeneration by the African is a familiar watchword and one that merits attention and consideration. He [Dr Blyden,] asserts that the cure for Africa is the American Negro. Methinks the experiment in Liberia has not proved to be such a decided success as to lead us to have confidence in it when tried on a larger scale. Like the Israelites of the Exodus, their [17] souls have not emerged from bondage, although their bodies are free. We must wait for all that generation from twenty years old and upwards at the time of the abolition to die off first ... even then I am doubtful of the result. There seems to be little or no enthusiasm for African regeneration on the part of the mass of the colored people, either in the States or the West Indies, or even in Liberia.

From the late distinguished Frederick Douglass,[22] of Washington, author of *My Bondage and My Freedom*[23] comes this vigorous and determined opposition to anything savoring of Negro colonization of Africa:

---

[20] 1st ed has "that" instead of "the".
[21] Alexander Mackay (1849-1890) served Uganda through the Church Missionary Society from 1878 until his death. For more on Mackay see J.W. Harrison, *A.M. Mackay, Pioneer Missionary of the C.M.S., Uganda*, (1890).
[22] Frederick Douglass (1817-1895) was born into slavery in Maryland. After escaping into freedom in 1838 he became a renowned abolitionist. His biography is: William S. Feely, *Frederick Douglass*, (New York: Norton, 1991).
[23] Douglass' second of three autobiographies, it gives the most detailed account of his life as a slave. (New York: Miller, Orton and Mulligan, 1855).

AFRICA FOR THE AFRICAN.

It is all nonsense to talk about the removal of eight millions of people to Africa. It would take more money than the cost of the late war to transport even one-half of the colored people of the United States to Africa.... The expense and hardships, to say nothing of the cruelty attending such a measure, would make success impossible.[24]

The former doubts the Negro's fitness to uplift the African; the latter seems to show his unwillingness to make the attempt; yet both are labouring and suffering for the African race.

Without combatting the opinion of either, let us consider the CHRISTIAN SETTLEMENT PROPOSAL; the basis of operation being somewhat as follows:

A. Each settlement to provide for ten families and to have a total land area of 2,000 acres, with a capital of £3,000 available. ($15,000).[25]

B. Each family to have allotted to them 200 acres of land and to have gradually available for its development the tenth[26] part of the capital: viz., £300 at the discretion of duly appointment superintendent.

C. Each settler to develop his own block for a period of seven years, under direction, for the benefit of the Union; he and his family being entitled to modest maintenance only during that period; the whole proceeds being the property of the Union till

---

[24] This quotation comes from a speech Douglass gave in 1892 and 93 and was first printed in the pamphlet, *The Lessons of the Hour* (Baltimore: Thomas & Evans, 1894) which has been recently reprinted in *The Oxford Frederick Douglass Reader*. ed. by William L. Andrews (Oxford University Press, 1996). This citation is found on 356-7 in the new volume. Booth's text differs slightly from the printed version of 1894.
[25] 1st ed does not have dollar equivalent.
[26] 1st ed has "seventh".

the close of the seven years' period, thenceforth to become the absolute property of the settler, together with all appliances; a title to be given by the Union accordingly.

Schedule D.[27] shows that each family should, as an average during the seven years' period, provide for a five-fold number of persons to follow, thus, in addition to themselves becoming the owners of a valuable little estate affording substantial help to the uplifting of their own people and country.

What might be looked for from this or an amended plan on similar lines during a twenty-eight years' period, that is four terms of seven years each?

[18] Considering the very great facilities which exist in certain parts of Africa for lucrative operations, the writer submits the following as well within the range of probability:

I. - By applying each £3000 of the assumed half of the parent capital available, on the basis indicated, the result should be the founding of 2,500 Christians settlements.
II. - These under careful superintendency, and so long as anything like present conditions prevail, should find little difficulty over the seven years' period of providing for a further five-fold party or 12,500 settlements containing 125,000 families.
III. - The process, carefully prosecuted to the end of the fourth term viz., to the end of the 28th year, shows a probable power, if such were needed, of thus transplanting and comfortably providing for a total of 15,625,000 families, or, allowing three souls per family, over 45 million persons. Schedule D. shows the details.

Whatever margin may be considered advisable to allow for contingences, the measure of power must be admitted to be great. It needs to be

---

[27] 1st ed incorrectly refers readers to Schedule C.

AFRICA FOR THE AFRICAN.

remembered that many Negro families are sufficiently wealthy to purchase their own estate when they see it to be to their interest to do so.

The writer would strongly urge that when the fund thus created should be no longer needed to aid returning Negroes, that it should then become available for the native African Christian on a like basis.

Objections Considered.

Many objections will doubtless present themselves to those interested: it may be well to consider and answer some of these.

As to the mission proposal:

Objection 1.-What proof is there that mission stations can at the same time spread the gospel and conduct self-supporting operations, and yet be successful in both departments?

Answer. The proof lies in the fact that this is now being done with comparative ease by the Zambesi Industrial Mission, by the Nyassa Industrial Mission in B.C. Africa, and by the Adventists' Industrial Mission in Matabeleland.

Objection 2.-But will the Negro be equal as a missionary to the European?

Answer. Opinions on this matter are likely to differ much amongst Europeans, but the writer is deeply convinced that the white [19] man will never bridge the gulf between himself and the native as the Negro can. The wide-spread conviction settles ultimately and finally upon the native, that the white men, good or bad, are agreed upon one thing; viz., to take their land from them, and no matter what the

AFRICA FOR THE AFRICAN.

missionary may say or teach they are believed to be in some sort of collusion, while talking of heavenly things, with those who are resolved to possess the land under their feet, and then tax them for living upon it. After the first blush of truthfulness is past and the convert acquires knowledge, the more he learns, the more he becomes convinced of this. The Negro is beyond this blighting suspicion and can become to the native as he settles among them what the white man never can.

Objection 3.-But what of his business capacity?

Answer. Properly inducted into his work there is no reason to doubt his equal ability. Certain it is that the native Christians themselves display great aptitude and ability to conduct industrial mission work successfully, both spiritually and otherwise. They are indeed too often dwarfed and undervalued, owing to latent prejudice even in missionaries.

Objection 4.-But what opportunities are there for preaching the gospel if industries and profit-making have to be studied?

Answer. The opportunities are probably greater at industrial stations than at purely preaching stations, since at the former there are daily in attendance some hundreds of workers who stay for a period of three to six months, and are daily under gospel teaching and influence.

Objection 5.-But why should the stations acquired with Europeans' money be given up absolutely into the African's or Negro's hands?

Answer. Because the native, as he sees the comforts and power the European gathers round him and studiously retains, can not get rid of the belief that the European has come there to help himself primarily, and not for the sole purpose of helping the African. The only thing that will convince them of a real desire to help them, is to retire and leave them in possession of their own stations to teach their own people. Not until we have done that and kept nothing for ourselves, shall we have given them Christ's measure - "pressed down and shaken together."[28]

[20] Let us consider now some of the objections to the Christian settlement proposals.

Objection 1.-The Negro is happy enough where he is. Why seek to disturb him?

Answer. It may be so. There is a contentment founded on ignorance or limited knowledge. If the Negro is happy under conditions where 150 to 200 yearly have been and are being lynched, owing to race hatred and ineffectual justice, it is because his buoyant nature can surmount disadvantages and bear unjust treatment which goes to prove that he is worthy of the effort to do him greater justice.

Objection 2.-But the Negro does not want to go. He wants to stay.

Answer. This may be true of those who have attained good positions[29]; and if such can not see they can better themselves and help their people by going, by all means let them do what, all things considered, they are satisfied is the best for the present and future. The same may be true of some of the poorer class, but most likely because they have no means of getting to understand with certainty, the great, immediate, and far reaching advantages to be

---

[28] This is the second reference to Luke 6:38. See note 10 on page 22.
[29] 1st edition has "attained to good positions".

AFRICA FOR THE AFRICAN.

gained. Thirty years ago the same was true of the British poor. They turned their backs upon Africa and their faces toward America; but now the advantages of only a small part of Africa, in the south, draw them by tens of thousands. At present, the vastness of Africa defies them to overtake it rapidly, and long before they do, not only the Negro, but the African native will awake to be reckoned with and their prior claims considered. Certain it is that the Negro people have a right to the offer of being returned to the land whence their progenitors were violently abstracted.

Objection 3.-But what good would result?

Answer. Distribute one-half of them in Christian settlements, fairly separated and moderately sustained and fostered during the transition period and they forthwith become a greater evangelizing and educational power than ordinary missions can become in a century beyond which they would become the employers, moulding and developing the African raw material, out of which would inevitably flow a mutually enriching stream of intercourse and commerce, with their foster parent, America, whose rightful ward they are.

[21] This then forms the twofold method by which the British and American Christians are invited to cooperate in the attempt to do justly by the Negro of America and the West Indies, as also the natives of Africa, and thus wipe out the stains of the past as well as the wrongs of appropriation in the present.

Who will help? who will take the life-pledge? Who will become subscribers? who will become unpaid advocates?

THE THIRD METHOD by which AFRICA for the AFRICAN may become an accomplished fact is in the hands of the Negro himself,

AFRICA FOR THE AFRICAN.

counting those of the West Indies with those of America, the number is about ten millions. Not withstanding the diverse attitude adopted by Negro leaders and well-wishers upon the subject, the writer submits as one who has taken some pains to become personally acquainted with the Negro as well as the African native, that the greatest good of the greatest number of the whole African race lies undoubtedly in their UNION ON SOME BASIS.

United, they are destined to become, and that quickly, a new power in the earth, TOO REAL, and MASSIVE to be any longer despised.

Their Union will speedily command that respect and equality of treatment which has been so grudgingly rendered and more often withheld. Separated and deprived of the mutual aid they are adapted to impart to each other, they must remain as at present, a broken and comparatively powerless people.

As a whole the Negro strikes the reflective observer of the African's present day needs as a divinely prepared people for a work also prepared of God.

Probably the GREATEST HOPE of Africa's millions lies in the power and the[30] fitness of the Negro to supply what they sorely lack, whilst on the other hand the GREATEST HOPE of the Negro probably lies in his imparting to the African his knowledge in exchange for a co-partnership in the great African estate. The one is rich and strong, but does not know it; the other knows the power of wealth, but has no rich estate from which to gather it, hence they are a kind of necessary counterpart to each other, SHAPED BY WHOM?

The African needs knowledge of an agricultural and commercial, as well as of an educational and spiritual character: the Negro has these to give in an important degree.

---

[30] 2nd ed adds "the" before fitness, where the 1st ed mistakenly has "no".

AFRICA FOR THE AFRICAN.

The African specially needs helpers and teachers, who will not become instrumental to, or contended spectators of the alienation of his country; the Negro, having the same right to his fatherland with the African, stands in a very different position to the European however well intentioned.

The African has a rich and resourceful country; the Negro has no country except where he has to strenuously battle against social ostracism, rack rents and keen-cut competition.

[22] The African needs leading, perhaps governing by those whose interests are identical with his own and who having no vital racial difference, can give him in word and deed the right hand of brotherhood. The Negro is the only one with these qualifications.

The Negroes' fore-fathers were borne from their homes and sold into a pitless[31] slavery "for evil," but the power of God has overruled the devices of wicked men and manifested His ability to frustrate with a High hand and outstretched arm, combinations of men bent on perpetuating evil. As in the past He has burst asunder the bands of wickedness and let the oppressed go free, so will it be in the future. HOW, WE KNOW NOT, but the power and purpose of God we know.

"Deep calleth unto deep,"[32] and as the Negro has drank the dregs of tyranny and has been humiliated to the last degree, may it not be that he has a destiny of blessing in the future commensurate with the slough through which he has passed? It must be so.

One of the most promising factors in the moulding of Africa's future by the Negro is the fact that to a certain extent, he has the strength of the American government behind him. America has held herself aloof during the scramble for Africa, though she might with a good show of

---

[31] 1st ed has piteous here.
[32] See Psalm 42:7.

AFRICA FOR THE AFRICAN.

reason, have put in a substantial claim for her African charge. The European conspiracy to carve and digest her African neighbor, America is clear of and will thus have an independent hand to play, and likely an important part to accomplish. When her Negro protege needs her protection when the reforming, inspiring, and upbuilding power of the Negro's knowledge comes to be felt by the inert mass of African latent strength and European feathers come to be ruffled thereby, then will come America's opportunity to cast her mantle of moral support around her aspiring offshoot and so change the painful memories of the past into those of gratitude in the future.

Certainly it is that whilst the Negro very properly seek to recover the vast African estate to which he is distinctly entitled, he should retain a vigorous hold of his rights and privileges as an American citizen.

The after reach of this possible, may we not hope probable, development, may come to be the diversion of Africa's commerce, in a large degree unto American channels.

The Negro therefore holds the key to Africa's future as no other people can. His position is unique.

Whilst this may be quite true, the question remains, will the Negro respond to his day of opportunity? Will he recognize it before the floodtide has passed or will he take his ease caring for none of these things?

At present his indifference to Africa's needs and claims is remarkable. Africa is almost a bugbear to the average Afro-American as he is now designated.

[22] The magnificent opportunities which make European governments eager to possess Africa, strange to say, the Negro does not trouble about; doubtless he does not realize them to be actual facts.

He has had Africa flung at him as his future dumping-ground and so fights shy of it. He has almost been threatened with transportation

AFRICA FOR THE AFRICAN.

there, till probably he has more fear of, or dislike to Africa than any other race of people. He regards it as the land of savages, swamps and fevers. The little that he knows of Africa is mainly of the Liberian settlement which has certainly been chosen in as trying and unhealthy a part of Africa as could well be found, close to the Equator, low-lying and with a heavy rain-fall, the correct conditions to ensure a malarious country.

He forgets that Africa stretches 5000 miles from North to South and consequently furnishes a wide range for choice of climate. Nor[33] is this all.

At present he is affected with certain maladies caught from his European neighbors. The 'color' distemper he has caught quite strongly and is apt to look askance with a "don't-know-you" expression on his poor African relations.

The European malady of individual aggrandizement he has taken in a serious degree and labours zealously "to lay up treasure on earth."[34] He is fond too of distinction and is generous in the use of prefixes and affixes to the disadvantages of the visitor not so distinguished; yet we do indeed need men of distinction among them; such as will past the standard of greatness set up by Him who said. "He that WOULD BE GREATEST among you, let him become THE SERVANT OF ALL."[35]

The writer (who learned from a 3 months visit in 1895 to Washington and Virginia)[36] is fully aware that generally speaking it is a sorry task, a sort of forlorn hope for an European to appeal to the Negro; the pendulum of distrust having in its reaction, swung overfar, and left the Negro brother in need of the gentle reminder:

---

[33] 1st ed has "Not".
[34] See Matthew 6:19.
[35] See Matthew 23:11 and parallel verses.
[36] For more on this trip, see Langworthy, *The Life of Joseph Booth*, 71, 77f.

AFRICA FOR THE AFRICAN.

"If ye have respect to persons, ye commit sin" - James 2:9. But be that as it may, God's messengers must deliver their burden, whether men will hear or forbear.

The sad feature is that the sum total of this ignorance, indifference, and prejudice may loose to the African race the possession of their earthly heritage. No other ten millions of people have before them at the present time such a magnificent and unique opportunity, of at once blessing others and elevating themselves from comparative obscurity and poverty to the position where they become the beneficent guides to a mighty people.

The reality of this danger is visible in so profound at thinker as the late Fredrick Douglass. He says:

> The worst thing perhaps about this colonization nonsense is that it tends to throw over the Negro a mantle of despair. It leads him to doubt the possibility of his progress as an American citizen.
>
> [24] It also encourages popular prejudice with the hope that by persecution or persuasion the Negro can be dislodged and driven from his natural home, while in the nature of the case he must stay here if for no other reason than he cannot well get away.[37]

Mr. Douglass furthermore states: "It has already been given out that if we do not go of our own accord we may be forced to go at the point of the bayonet."

No wonder that dwelling in the midst of an overpowering number of white men who could contemplate such coercive measures, that an

---

[37] Frederick Douglass, *The Lessons of the Hour* reprinted in *The Oxford Frederick Douglass Reader*. ed. by William L. Andrews, 356-7. Booth's text differs slightly from the printed version of 1894.

AFRICA FOR THE AFRICAN.

inveterate hatred of African colonization schemes should be rooted in the Negro mind. But he[38] must look beyond this and not allow his vision to become blurred by the inconsiderate proposals of any parties.

He must get at the facts and weigh the evidence. If he goes to Africa or any other country it must be at his OWN CHOICE and for the greater good of his people, not to gratify others.

The true point of consideration for the Negro is whether America or Africa offers the largest measure of opportunity to bless and uplift the growing number of Negroes as well as bring good to the African.

Let us for a short time contrast some of the opportunities presented by America and Africa respectively for the poorer classes. Mr. Douglass shall again state the American case. He says:

> The land-owners of the South want the labour of the Negro on the hardest terms possible. They once had it for nothing. They now want it for next to nothing. To accomplish this they have contrived three ways. The first is to rent their land to the Negro at an exorbitant price per annum and compel him to mortgage his crop in advance to pay his rent.
>
> The landlord has a first claim upon everything produced upon the land. The Negro can have nothing; can keep nothing, can sell nothing without the consent of the landlord.... The landlord keeps books; the Negro does not, hence, no matter, how hard he may work, or how hard-saving he may be, he is, in most cases, brought in debt at the end of the year and once in debt he is fastened to the land as by hooks of steel.
>
> Another way, which is still more effective, is the practice of paying the labourer with orders on the store instead of with lawful money. By this means money is kept out of the hands of the Negro, and the Negro is kept entirely in the hands of the

---

[38] 1st ed has "the Negro".

AFRICA FOR THE AFRICAN.

landlord. He cannot save money because he gets none to save. He cannot seek a better market for his labor, because he has no money with which to pay his fare, and because he is by that vicious order system already in debt and therefore already in bondage.[39]

We shall hope that these conditions prevail only in a limited degree and only amongst the agricultural class.

[25] Though the writer's personal knowledge of the Negro's real position in the Southern States is of a limited nature, he does claim to have a personal and particular knowledge of some of the many opportunities existing in South Africa, East Africa and East Central Africa.

South Africa, that is, south of the river Zambesi and its parallel on the west coast, though very rich in gold, diamonds and agricultural resources over a large part of its surface, is not for the present recommended to the Negro as offering the greatest opportunities. Its merits or demerits will be formed at a later page. In passing, it may, however, be said that there may be powerful ultimate reasons why the American Negro should resolve to make himself at home in South Africa and its affairs.

North of the Zambesi the position and opportunities, present and future are very different. It is not too much to say that if there were fifty millions of Negroes, needing a home and an ample, fertile and a comparatively healthy one, the Zambesi and the water system it is the key to afford a certain and abundant opportunity. Here the conditions are more ripe and favorable to take a solid grip of Central Africa than by the great Western entrance to the heart of Africa; viz., the Congo River. The tide of European power in its more oppressive aspects, with

---

[39] Frederick Douglass, *The Lessons of the Hour* reprinted *in The Oxford Frederick Douglass Reader*, 359-360.

AFRICA FOR THE AFRICAN.

its ill-conceived aversions[40] to the African race, is here as yet but faintly felt. Long may that tide be restrained. The fragrance of the confidence inspired by such good men as Dr. Livingstone[41] and his immediate missionary followers has not yet been fully destroyed. The treatment the Zulu receives at the hands of the British and Dutch is unknown to and unbelievable by them. The distance of twelve to fifteen[42] miles separates them besides several, to them, unknown tongues; and so the white man is not burdened with the record of the past, and the simple native largely trusts himself and his country in the European's hands, watching with intelligent wonder the revelations of his superior knowledge, assuming that such bestows on the European unknown and unlimited rights. His charming simplicity plays into the Europeans' hands. The latter might have dealt nobly by his trustful brother in black, but so far, he certainly has not, and the writer, as one Englishman, confesses with shame, that we have, as a people, been TRIED IN THE BALANCES and so far are FOUND WANTING.

Whether this shall continue to be the verdict remains with the Christians of Great Britain to say.

The spirit of God demands that we shall not rob these, his little children, of their land and liberty. If we continue to do so, He will lift up a standard against us in His own time and way, perchance, striking from our hands the Power[43] and leaving us only in the possession of the guilt.

---

[40] 1st ed has "aversion" (singular).
[41] David Livingstone (1813-73), the missionary and explorer of Central Africa, served with the London Missionary Society from 1841-1856. He believed that civilization could be brought to Africa through a combination of Christianity and legitimate commerce which would bring an end to the slave trade. For more on Livingstone, see G. Seaver, *David Livingstone, His Life and Letters* (London: 1957).
[42] 1st ed has 1500, which seems more appropriate here.
[43] 1st ed does not capitalize power.

AFRICA FOR THE AFRICAN.

Within the part of Central Africa occupied by the British crown since the year 1890 and called the British Central African Protectorate, the land is now sold at half a crown, or sixty cents per acre. It can also be leased for [26] a period of years at eight per cent of its freehold value; viz: 2d. per acre, per year.

Native labor costs at present about 3s., or about 70 cents per month for agricultural or plantation work. The net profits to be realized per acre are consequently larger than can be expected to continue[44] for very many years.

Coffee is giving a net gain of £10, £15, and £20 per acre, according to the ability with which the plantation is managed. Sugar, maize and cotton will be likely to average £10 or $50[45] per acre, one season with another.

Outside the British sphere and in the country they are distinctly pledged not to enter, some hundreds of millions of acres remain in the possession of the native owners who are willing to sell to *persons they approve*, large blocks at a cost of one to two cents per acre, according to circumstances and locality.

This land is equal to the higher priced British land but is not favored with such doubtful advantages as that rule affords: it may in some sections be slightly more remote, but not to an appreciable extent. The Negro here would not only be the land-owner, but the employer and benefactor; for there are at each new settlement hosts of applicants for work in order to secure the twelve yards of calico per month he so much prizes. The people are splendid people to work with and gladly adopt the new life where some payment is given for the work done.

---

[44] 1st ed has "or continued" instead of "to continue".
[45] 1st ed has $50, but 2nd ed mistakenly has £50.

AFRICA FOR THE AFRICAN.

As proof of what is being done, the writer ventures to record that on two blocks of land he purchased direct from a native chief four years ago and which cost in calico less than one cent per acre, are now yielding 5 cwt. or about 600 pounds of coffee per acre, which realizes in London 90s. per cwt., leaving a net profit of over £15 or $75 per acre. These are now mission property. The climate is good. The summers are not nearly as hot as in Virginia, America; the winters are mild, dry and delightful; the transport of produce is cheap and the cost of living very small.

The population, as elsewhere stated, within the British sphere (and this is the portion most developed) is about one European to each 3000 natives. Outside this section, but north of the Zambesi river, the proportion is approximately one European to 8,000 natives, as the following brief summary will show.

North of the Zambesi.

	Europeans.	Natives.
British Central African Protectorate,	289	844,420.
South African Chartered Co,	20	about 2,500,000.
Portuguese,	about 500	2,000,000.
British Imperial East Africa, do	250	2,000,000.
	1,059	7,344,420.[46]

[27] Strange to relate, the revenue in the recently created B.C.A. Protectorate has risen from nothing in 1890 to £51,000[47] in 1895-6, largely owing to the hut tax, which as yet is only mildly imposed and that over a part of the country. Allowing four persons per hut (though three would be more correct) there are 211,105[48] poor native grass

---

[46] 1st ed has incorrect math with a total of 8,344,420.
[47] 1st ed has £51,400
[48] 1st ed has 633,315

AFRICA FOR THE AFRICAN.

huts to impose this tax upon and gradually increase it as the custom is up to ten or twelve shillings. The Zulus pay 14s. per hut, so that when the hold is strong enough to demand a ten s. tax, these simple trustful people will contribute £105,052,[49] yearly for the doubtful privilege of handing their country over to the astute European to sell and indeed do what he likes with using these same persons as the instruments of labor to extract and pass over its wealth.

To an observer who reflects upon the position and has been reared in an atmosphere of justice, the picture is distracting. He sees these same natives who have quietly submitted to their land being sold block after block to the planter by the government consul, sent at will by some authority to go fight and slay any tribe that ventures to question the orthodoxy of this process: and such is the simplicity of these people that they consider that having themselves began to pay this tax as a sign of their vassalage to the unknown wonderful white queen, they must forthwith go and kill for 5d. or 6d. per day any tribe of their people they are told to fight, and thus by means of the very tax they themselves pay, furnishing the means for imposing the same bondage upon other wondering[50] tribes and dispossessing them in turn of the land the philanthropic European commissioner is ready to sell to the first comer at the tempting figure of 2s. 6d. per acre. The native spoken to and asked what he thinks of this process (if he can trust the inquirer) says plainly he dare not refuse, or he expects the white chief would turn the war upon his people instead. The tax he does not mind so much, but going to rob others of their land and put them under the tax of the

---

[49] It is likely that the figure is a printer's error. There are 20 shillings to the pound, so given 211,105 huts paying 10 shillings each, the total would result in 2,111,050 shillings or £105,552.5 (£105,552 and 10s). The 1st ed has £105,502,100, which suggests that the printer probably misread the last 5 as a 0 and mistook 10s. for 100. The second edition neglects to correct the figure.
[50] This should probably read "wandering".

distant queen, this he detests, but he must do it when told; for where is there even a white man who dare refuse to do his bidding?

A noble instance of natives who preferred imprisonment to this process the writer met at a Chinde[51], on the Zambesi River. Here are three Ajawa prisoners, by name, Mponda, Chipalamaba and Kumsumala. These are three small Ajawa chiefs from near Lake Nyassa[52]. These being good fighting men, and the Portuguese Commandante, having heard of their prowess, approached them by permission of the late vice consul, Mr. King, with an offer of liberty if they would go and fight for them. Their answer was, "We cannot fight our brothers who are trying to save their land as we ourselves did; no, we can die in prison, but we can not do that." Other three prisoners of the same Ajawa tribe the writer saw at Port Herald[53], Shire River, who pitifully lifted up their chained hands and asked; "Now that the white queen has got their land and all they had, could they not have their freedom once more? their power was gone, and their white masters are[54] strong."

[28] The crime of all these was that they had sold slaves to get weapons and ammunition in order, so they state, to prevent their land from being stolen. The curious question is thus raised: is it necessary in order to rebuke chiefs for slave-selling, that their land and that of all their people shall be taken from them and they themselves put under permanent taxation and vassalage to the supposed British protector? And is it necessary when this extreme penalty has been paid to keep such overpunished offenders as these six small sub-chiefs in prison and chains? Is this the British generosity believed in school-boy days, to be the portion of Britain's fallen foe?

---

[51] A British concession harbor at the mouth of the Zambesi.
[52] Now known as Lake Malawi.
[53] Now Nsanje in Southern Malawi.
[54] 1st ed has "were".

AFRICA FOR THE AFRICAN.

A shudder of shame and sorrow is begotten at the discovery of how little the spirit of Christianity[55] permeates our National doings amongst a helpless people.

Whilst in the territory marked off as British, the proportion of Europeans is one to each 3,000 natives, outside these boundaries the ratio is 1 to each 8,000 natives. Here the European commends himself to the African by more amiable and harmless operations. If the new-comer is a missionary, his good words soon ensure him a welcome. If a gold-seeker and adventurer or a hunter, he is well armed with presents with which to win his way till his foothold becomes strong enough to warrant less conciliatory measures. The good-natured African either charmed by the gentle peace assuring words of the missionary, or by the tempting presents of the adventurer soon affords the white man a place, admiring his knowledge and believing in his good intentions. His amiability and trustful readiness to adopt civilization and quit the old life, lead him to yield the supremacy to the white man. What has happened to distant tribes, he is strangely ignorant of by reason of the difference of language and the absence of intercourse.

It is an awful conclusion to have forced into one's soul, but it seems to be the sorrowful fact, that the European is so intensely selfish, that he is, as a race utterly incapable of doing justice to his fellow men whom God has chosen to create with black skins.

One ought doubtless not to despair, for God is yet able to move mightily upon this generation of exploiters, cause them to consider and reform their ways ere His vengeance overtakes them.

Let the righteous pray and work for this. In the meantime, let the Negro also do his part and make the African's case his own in a way the European never can. The writer would urge these to a study of

---

[55] **1st ed has Christ.**

AFRICA FOR THE AFRICAN.

SOUTH AFRICAN DOINGS

During the past thirty years, in order that they may better estimate the possibilities of the coming thirty years in the Virgin country first referred to. Then, states and colonies that had no existence or were just struggling [29] to take a form, are today able to record their revenue by hundreds of thousands, and in three instances by millions of pounds sterling.

Then their white populations were small. Today they have reached the position of being one-tenth of the entire population, the remaining nine parts being native Africans. See the following:

Revenue of

British:	∎Cape Colony,	6,828,000 Pounds Sterling
	∎Natal,	1,169,780
	∎Zululand,	43,667
Dutch:	∎Transvaal,	3,539,955
	∎Free State,	408,551
	∎Basutoland,	44,627
	∎Amatongaland,	
British:	∎South African Company,	44,489
	∎British C. Africa Protectorate,	51,400
	∎Bechuanaland,	62,000
Portuguese East Africa,		194,896
German West Africa[56],		10,000
		£12,396,365

---

[56] The numbers here suggest that Booth probably meant German East Africa, which was comprised of what is now mainland Tanzania. Having never been to West Africa, Booth would have known little about German West Africa, which would refer to present day Togo and Cameroon.

AFRICA FOR THE AFRICAN.

Since the Emancipation of the American slaves the revenue of these small sections of Africa has increased over twelve millions of pounds sterling, that is about sixty millions of dollars yearly. No small sum of this is from the Native hut tax, but gold and diamonds have during the past twenty years made most of the difference.

The present proportions of the white and native populations south of the Zambesi river is worth noting; the underwritten are taken from government records, excepting in two instances:

Population of South Africa, South of Zambesi in the Sections named:

	Whites	Natives
BRITISH:-		
CAPE COLONY	386,812	1,385,620
NATAL	42,759	469,747
ZULULAND	850	163,447
SOUTH AFRICAN CHARTERED COMPANY	4,843 (about)	2,000,000
		10 to sq. mile
BASUTOLAND	578	250,000
AMATONGALAND	100	40,000
[30] BECHUANALAND	12,726	386,200
BECHUANALAND CROWN COLONY	---	57,472
DUTCH:-		
TRANSVAAL	165,000	605,000
ORANGE FREE STATE	80,717	129,787
PORTUGUESE	800 (10 to sq m)	150,000
GERMAN SOUTH AFRICA[57]	1,000	117,000
	693,185	7,103,673[58]

---

[57] Booth probably meant German South West Africa, now Namibia.
[58] Figures do not add up. Totals should be 696,185 and 5,754,273

AFRICA FOR THE AFRICAN.

The Natives are therefore ten times as numerous as the Europeans in the most populated part of Africa.

Certain authorities publish their opinion that this section of Africa south of the Zambesi parallel, would comfortably provide for 320,000,000 of people without being over-crowded.

This is worked out in the following manner: The Cape District, which has a population of 257 persons to the square mile. If then, the remaining country South of the Zambesi should ever come to be equally densely populated, it would, from its known area, contain the large number of 321,250,000. (Large portions being badly watered, one third of this total is not likely to be exceeded.)

The INDUCEMENTS of South Africa, it has already been said, are not, ON THE SURFACE of things, attractive to the Negro or colored man of any cast; especially, if he is, in whatever degree of African blood.

An infusion of the irrepressible Negro of the Douglass type would however be of inestimable value to the fast awakening South African native and would likely create some interesting changes in their treatment and position during the coming years.

But generally speaking, the supercilious and oppressive attitude assumed by the majority of South African whites to their black brethren is too marked to give the pliable Negro a moderate chance. Only strong resolute men, prepared to do and bear something for the race should go there, and as Mr. Douglass says, these are perhaps needed most in America, if there is as much to be gained there.

The Negroes' labor, however skillful, will rarely command more than one-third or one-half that of a white man of equal ability.

In the Dutch Country[59] the statute law is that a native or Negro shalt NEVER HAVE EQUALITY IN CHURCH OR STATE with the European; a lie

---

[59] Transvaal and the Orange Free State.

AFRICA FOR THE AFRICAN.

that shall one day break up the Republic that has dared to incorporate a law so offensive and contrary to the law of God and God fearing men. It may be taken as settled that since they have thus chosen to measure their strength deliberately against the word of God, their days of power are numbered. [31] The present, with over a million pounds surplus, is their day of seeming power, but time will reveal God's dealings with Nations who boast themselves and oppress the weak.

In Johannesburg, their chief city, the punishment for a Negro who dares to walk on the foot-path is the lash, the prison, or fine. A badge of humility must be worn on the arm, denoting whose servants they are, for they MUST recognize someone as their master.

In Natal, (British), for the Native to be out of his "location", after the ringing of a kind of Curfew bell, is to be liable to imprisonment with hard labor as a convict; the time this bell is rung is 9 o'clock in some, and 8 o'clock in other parts.

In Bechuanaland,[60] the country is practically ruled by the African Chief Kahma, a staunch Christian convert. Here a greatly improved state of things exists and some regard to the rights of the black man is given, but for these exemptions and privileges, Kahma has had to make a vigorous stand.[61]

Recently his country was about to have given over to the tender mercies of the South African Chartered Company and the free circulation

---

[60] Now Botswana.

[61] Chief Kgama III (c.1835-1923) was baptized in 1860 and assumed the chieftaincy of Ngato, in North East Bechuanaland, in 1875, ruling until his death. His diplomatic skill saved his people from annexation by the Boer Republics and the British South African Company, and his adherence to Christianity and his acceptance of British rule led him to be accepted as a leader of his people by white missionaries and government officials. J.M. Chirenje, *Chief Kgama and His Times c.1835-1923: The Story of a Southern African Ruler,* (London: Rex Collings, 1978), 107-8.

AFRICA FOR THE AFRICAN.

of drink amongst the people. This God-fearing chief, believing in the righteousness of his cause and in the divine power, to deliver him and his people went to Britain and throughout the whole country appealed to large gatherings of the people who flocked to hear him, to do him justice, keep out from his land the drink curse and leave him with a fair measure of power, subject to the oversight of the British Crown, not of a[62] Company of men whose actions have already produced such a legacy of hatred in the hearts of the neighboring Mashona, Matabele and Makalaka tribes. To the lasting honor of the British leaders then in power and to the populace, who heard and heartily responded to this voice from Africa, be it recorded that the requests acceded to[63], consequently Bechuanaland must be regarded as exempt in the main from the indictment brought by the writer in some humble way against Britain and her doings in Africa.

What has been conceded to Bechuanaland and its noble chief is urgently requested for the other sections under British rule.

Basutoland[64], a small protectorate of about 10,000 square miles is a remarkable case of exemption from the grasping policy complained of.

It has not been handed over to the tender mercies of the soul-less public companies, or yet to the control of the all devouring colonist.

The land has not been sold for revenue purposes and the people gradually rendered servile to the point of intimidation.

Its land has been preserved for the people who cultivate it in a superficial manner on a sort of commonweal principal[65] under the direction of their chiefs; and cannot, as yet, be bought by the white man. These

---

[62] 1st ed does not have "a" here.
[63] 1st ed has "requests accorded to".
[64] Booth later spent a short time in Basutoland (now Lesotho). See Langworthy, *The Life of Joseph Booth*, Chapter 28.
[65] The meaning here is principle.

AFRICA FOR THE AFRICAN.

chiefs practically administer the country under the control of an Imperial British resident.

[32] The mineral resources of the country have been preserved. The people pay a 10s. hut tax and have been protected from the white incursion of drink-sellers and gold-hunters. The British Government hold THE RESERVE POWER to continue this protection and at the same time develop the latent resources of the country by the people and for the people and ultimately RESTORE the land fully to the people. Will it be done?

The Basutus are a suitable people and the existing governmental conditions are favorable for the enlightened development, in a Christian progressive spirit, of the substantial resources at present largely dormant in both people and land, for the greatest good of the African, retaining no more for the European than the reimbursement for the necessary and economical outlay incurred.

Then would probably be accomplished what Sir H.H. Johnston, late administrator of the Central African Protectorate, so clearly defines and has seriously attempted, viz.

> The education of the black people into a state dependent on the British Empire in matters of general policy and thrown open unrestrictedly to British trade enterprise.

This is the position for the great tracts of territory at present in the disposition of the British Crown, viz:

1. The Central African Protectorate.
2. Imperial British East Africa.
3. The whole territory claimed by the British South African Chartered Company, otherwise occasionally called "Rhodesia".
4. The Royal Niger Company's territory in West Africa.

AFRICA FOR THE AFRICAN.

NATIVE LOCATIONS.

Returning now to the subject of the "locations," provided for the South African Natives. Let the casual visitor pay a visit to several of these, say easily reached ones as those adjacent to the sea-port towns of East London, Port Elizabeth and Durban, and observe what a Christian people have provided in the way of accommodation for the people whose land they have seized to erect their own comfortable structures upon. At these and similar towns of importance, the visitor will find the native has been studiously excluded from the power to even purchase a plot of land for native use. At East London, (almost within sight of the costly structures provided for the European), 40 foot square allotments, for which he must pay a high rental, (the 12s. hut tax) and be liable to "move on" at his own cost at any time when his presence is no longer desired. At Port Elizabeth, he will find the Negro still more miserably housed (with just[66] a few exceptions) in shelters, not houses or huts even, built of packing-case linings and crammed into a miserably small square, a disgrace to every official or Town Councillor, [33] or Minister or Christian of the place; as well as a disgrace to any British system of government that can first appropriate and then inconsiderately make such heartless provision for the poor people it has stripped and left helpless.

At Durban he will find the Native huts pushed[67] away out of sight into a kind of barracks, where he is crammed into - to him, disgustingly close contact with a horde of imported Hindu coolies, whom his soul abhors as another kind of invader of his country in the way of competive labor and a candidate for the land of his fathers. (These poor Hindoos have a long list of real grievances against the planters to whom they are bound for a five years' period under the indenture sys-

---

[66] 1st ed has "first" in place of "just".
[67] 1st ed does not have "pushed".

AFRICA FOR THE AFRICAN.

tem. These are being presented exhaustively by one of their number to the government authorities in India.)

This "barracks," or "location" at Durban is a fair synopsis of the European proposals and purposes toward the black man.

It starts by putting him at arm's length from European society. It despises him for being ignorant, but resolutely keeps him so.

It takes his land at first gently, smilingly, and imperceptibly, then forcibly when the African is rude enough to object; and afterwards hires back to him the smallest possible portion in the least valuable position at a substantial rental or tax, but reserving the right to terminate even such tenancy at will. It admires his brute strength and carefully calculates how little he can maintain this on and how much he can by ingenious pressure, suited to the modern conscience, be brought to expend this at the lowest rate of remuneration, in aid of the wealth making projects of his conquerers.

It speaks in laudatory terms of the "Raw Kaffir," as contrasted with the bespoiled and hopelessly ruined "Mission black" or otherwise educated Native.

It fears his acquisition of knowledge lest he discovers his real strength and right and at the same time unmasks the hypocritical cant of the Christian profession, which passes sanctimoniously or jauntily by on the fashionable "other side," or at best, makes a dainty fingered accurately doctrined declaration of a gospel of Brotherhood and good will;[68] to the obligations of which it cleverly and perseveringly turns an averted gaze. It has at length made the charming discovery how to serve "God and Mammon," and what can be wished for more?

Talk to these Natives, as the writer has done, and ask them why come there to be packed like herrings in a barrel, with no decent space for

---

[68] 1st ed has "goodly will".

unavoidable human needs, and they will tell you that they would not come to that place where they will be made convicts of, if out of the "location" after bell-ringing at night; and in the day are cuffed, cursed and driven by their white employers, while loading or unloading ships or other laborious work, but they are forced to come to earn the [34] 14 shilling hut tax they pay to possess in peace the grass huts they call home.

At a hired house, a stone's throw from this location, the writer had a curious and never-to-be-forgotten meeting with about 100 of the best educated native converts, (Zulus) sent from different Districts by appointment as Christian delegates. At 10 a.m. on the morning of Oct. 7th, 1896, they began to gather and at 10:30 a.m., NEXT DAY, they dispersed, never stopping night or day during 24 and a half hours the record of their charges of wrongs sustained at the hands of the British.

Upon the one English listener, these fell like an avalanche, for many were manifestly unanswerable charges. Their many-sided indictments summed up, amounted to this, there was no white man known to the Zulu people worthy of absolute trust, no missionary, no legislator, no civilian, No, NOT ONE.[69] The last honest white man was dead, and that was "Sobantu", the man who loved the people, viz: the late Bishop Colenso.[70]

---

[69] This could be a reference to Romans 3:10f, "there is none righteous, no, not one", referring back to the 14th Psalm.
[70] John William Colenso (1814-1883) was appointed the first bishop of the Anglican diocese of Natal in 1853. He earned the Zulu name "Sobantu", which means "father of the people", for his dedication to the rights of the Africans. Like Booth, Colenso urged the British government to treat Africans justly and grant the Africans among whom he ministered independence. Adrian Hastings, *The Church in Africa 1450-1950*, (Oxford: Clarendon, 1994). For more on Colenso, see G.W. Cox, *The Life of Bishop Colenso*, (2 vols., London, 1888).

AFRICA FOR THE AFRICAN.

One speaker, perfectly master of the English tongue, said: "Their country was a home no longer, but a spacious prison, for move which way they would, they were met with a demand for a passport on every side. For the Missionary's education they were very thankful, but it only revealed to them that even they were more or less, in willing or compulsory collusion with their oppressors."

And so the writer left that painfully oppressive locality burdened with a forecast of the Great-African-many-voiced-accusation which awaits the heedless European of this age in the day God has appointed for the judgement of all men.

A few weeks later, the writer being en route for England, called at the Island of St. Helena, Napoleon's prison and final resting place. At the gate-way, nailed to a tree, he was startled by seeing a proclamation board notifying under the heading, "Zulu Notice," that a penalty of £20 would indicated upon any visitor speaking to any of the Zulu prisoners on the Island without the Governor's permission; yet these were free to walk about as they pleased and mix with the populace. The permission was duly[71] applied for and freely granted.

The prisoners proved to be two brothers and a son of the late famous Cetewayo, the son's name being "Dinizulu." There were also two sub-chiefs or "Indunas." One of the brothers of Cetewayo, the younger, was a particularly fine, impressive, good-natured, noble-looking young man, worthy apparently, of a better fate. By means of their guardian, a Zulu interpreter, a pleasant chat was held for a few minutes by the writer and a Native Christian African friend[72] from the Ajawa tribe of Central Africans. To see a genuine black stranger seemed to cheer their hearts; though their respective native languages were hopelessly unintelligible to each other.

---

[71] 1st edition has "only".

[72] Langworthy suggests that this companion may have been John Chilembwe who was en route to America with Booth. *The Life of Joseph Booth*, 93.

AFRICA FOR THE AFRICAN.

[35] The few minutes' talk revealed the same deep-seated conviction that there was no hope of generous treatment from the white race of men. "Their[73] words were sweet, but their deeds were bitter." They were polite, guarded and distrustful, but in no way resentful of the intrusion.

Surely with their former country in the possession of 43,609 British and 242,716 Europeans in the Dutch portion, Great Britain can afford to consider the heart-yearnings of these conquered and helpless foes, (whatever their past record may have been) for a grass hut once again in their native land!! Even as a poor matter of policy, is it not worth considering, what a pulsation of gratitude and satisfaction would thrill through the whole Zulu people to find the British HAD HEARTS, after all?

But can it not be done from the nobler motives and in faith that GOOD and not evil shall result from a good and generous act?

Returning, however, to the consideration of the native locations, what shall be said of the compounds we find at such mining towns as Kimberly and Johannesburg but that they act as a kind of jibbet, bringing out in to bold relief the ingenious heartlessness to which the modern spirit of greed can descend in its exploitation of African ignorance and helplessness. Whether we look at the government, the mining capitalists or the planter class the spirit is the same. The complaints of cruelty of the planter on the tea and sugar plantations of Natal are very numerous and find their way in various forms into public notice. The following is a letter from one of these written in the spirit of self justification, for it is astonishing how soon the old barbarous spirit reasserts itself as soon as men get a little power over a weaker people. It is taken from the *Natal Advertiser* of the 5th of September 1896:

---

[73] Both editions misspelled this word "There".

AFRICA FOR THE AFRICAN.

My experience of natives convinces me they area bad lot. They must be kept down with a strong hand. Attempts to Christianize them have proved worse than useless. The school Kaffir almost invariably turns out a blackguard. Our legislature ought to re-assert the right of every white man to whollop his own nigger. I would not give a single penny to the cause of missions.... No good preaching the gospel to these creatures. I hardly think they can have souls. At any rate, if they have, they are NOT WORTH SAVING.

Yet, in a country where so much of an aggravating nature is endured by the Zulu people, the native population is rather more than ten times the number of their European conquerors, a strong testimony to their peaceful character, entitling them to a more considerate treatment.

Between this part and the Zambesi River, there lies

The Matabele and Mashona Country,[74]

a stretch of about 500 miles northward. This is said to be largely gold bearing, and consequently, is claimed by an English company of speculators [36] who have bought it up from certain adventurers who have purchased favor with unsuspecting chiefs by means of presents, etc., and thus acquired concessions which were usually Greek and incomprehensible to the grantors of them. This company, whose claims rest upon such curiously laid foundation, asserts the right to a large territory, reported to be 750,000 square miles, or 480 millions of acres in extent. Once grant, as a safe basis of procedure, that the native African "has no rights that the white man is bound to respect," and this stupendous claim may be[75] taken as just. But as this principle is not yet fully established, this assumed territory of this remarkable company is best reckoned[76] as qualifiable by a large note of interrogation.

---

[74] This area is in Zimbabwe today.
[75] 1st ed does not have "be".
[76] 1st ed has "auctioned" in place of "reckoned".

AFRICA FOR THE AFRICAN.

The methods by which the Matabele and Mashona tribes have been hoodwinked and gradually deprived of their possessions is carefully exposed in a pamphlet published by the Aborigines' Protection Society of London, dated January, 1897.[77] The fact that this company's employees have adopted a heartless "shoot at sight"[78] policy toward the native is exposed[79].

The British Crown, we must hope, is not answerable for this company's treatment of the natives of the country. Their agents hire by the hundred, bodies of men, mostly new arrivals seeking work of some kind, at the rate of 5s. to 10s.[80] per day and food, to go and shoot down the people who object to their process of acquiring the land. This is called "war", and the natives who object to be shot or hanged by these visitors, (shall we not say manslayers?) are called "rebels;" yet they are simply defending, as every European would, their homes from destruction and their women from outrage.

The writer has met, stayed with, traveled with and accused certain of these hired man-slaughterers. Their soulless answer generally is, that it was "only niggers" they shot or hanged to the nearest tree, and "what good are niggers?"

The natives who thus manifest their views of this further encroachment are sufficiently near their Zulu neighbors, conquered by the British and Dutch, to comprehend the fate that awaits them, and apparently prefer[81] to die in defence of their land and liberty rather than to submit to a civilization and taxation presenting so loathsome a garb of "take all and give nothing."

---

[77] 1st ed has "in the early part of 1897".
[78] 1st ed has "short of sight".
[79] 1st ed has "made manifest".
[80] 1st ed has 6s.
[81] 1st edition has "to prefer".

AFRICA FOR THE AFRICAN.

Who shall say their choice, TILL WE MEND OUR METHODS, is not a wise one?

The Negro reader will thus see why, to the average individual of his people, seeking release from the racial conflict which has so long been his portion, combined with the search for improved financial prospects, South Africa does not offer the most attractive field.

Yet viewed from a more important standpoint, namely, the greatest good to the greatest number of the whole African race, it should be the [37] very distinct policy of Negro thought leaders, whilst holding every inch of their present foothold in America, to direct their surplus forces to a union policy with the many sections of the great African family in this, their day of need.

The important preparatory work which has been accomplished by generous and disinterested mission work in South Africa; the banishment or weakening of tribal jealousies and distrust; the rendering accessible of the native mind and heart by the acquisition of his language and the imparting to him of the English tongue; the conscious need of the awakening African of qualified and unbiased leaders of mature experience, and with an appreciable affinity to their own race; the turning hopelessly from the white man as a deliverer; the visible yearning for aid from those who are at once familiar with, and up to the present date with the curious and diversified genuflections of European thought, purpose, power or prejudice, and at the same time are "bone of their bone, flesh of their flesh and skin of their skin"[82] (as recently expressed by a Zulu); the visible richness and salubrity of South Africa, together with the accessibility and vastness of its yet to be developed resources; the existing mixed European governments of a conflicting character and with antagonistic purposes ill concealed; their varying degrees of unsatisfactory or oppressive treatment of natives;

---

[82] See Genesis 2:23.

AFRICA FOR THE AFRICAN.

the great numerical majority the latter at present maintain, and the power this ultimately foreshadows by means of equal voting rights or otherwise; the possible developments of the future as the existing heterogeneous elements revolve or ripen: these and kindred considerations should cause intelligent Negroes to devise methods by which they will get in touch with and keep in touch with African interests, rights and possibilities in South Africa, whilst taking equal care that the less complex and, probably, vaster opportunities existing in other parts of Africa are courageously and believingly availed of.

Little has been said of the openings presented in Western Africa, the conditions there not being at present so inviting for immediate operations; nor is the climate so healthy as in the sections more particularly considered.

If the writer is asked, "how can a beginning be made?" by those Negro friends whose interest is sufficiently aroused, he would say, (if no better plan be forthcoming,) let such enter upon and carry out the programme as before defined in the European portion of this appeal. Let them also consider with care and patience the proposed basis of the African Christian Union, and if they consider it wise, form[83] a DISTINCTLY SEPARATE Negro or Afro-American Christian Union with such amendments or excisions as their experience indicates. By all means, let that be done and done quickly; for the work is great and the time is short but God is able and nothing is too hard if He wills it to prosper.

[38] Let the call be long and loud and clear in the name of Jesus Christ, the son of God, with power. Not only to the European but to every one with any tinge of African blood coursing through his veins,

THIS DAY TO DO HIS DUTY

---

[83] 1st edition has "to form" instead of the comma followed by "form".

AFRICA FOR THE AFRICAN.

and unite their strength in faith that God is waiting to bless the great African race in ways which He will, in His time, reveal.

Let those Christians that are sensible that the spirit of God would have them move in this matter, nominate their own treasurer, secretary and executive board.

Let every woman and child, as far as able, who have blood relationship to the African race, resolve to take some living part in the work of Africa's redemption.

Let the doubters and half hearted stand aside till they have found a better way.

Let all be aware of the folly and danger of an easy, do-nothing policy, and let such as can not or do not care to help, be not guilty of hindering those who are willing.

Let those pray who can not give.

Let those pray who give also.

Let those who give and pray search earnestly for others who will do likewise.

Let prayer unions be formed to ensure God's blessing upon the work and all connected with it.

Let those who wish to offer their lives for the work at home or in Africa, make known their desire to the secretary when appointed.

Let women and girls take part and form a Woman's League, or Sister's League, as an auxiliary effort to aid their African sisters.[84]

There is no time to be lost: Africa's millions are awakening from the long slumber of heathen darkness. Who will extend to them a brother's guiding hand?

---

[84] "to aid their African sisters" was added in the second edition.

AFRICA FOR THE AFRICAN.

Let the African, sympathetically led by his more experienced Afro-American brother, develop his own country, establish his own manufactures, work his own plantations, run his own ships, work his own mines, educate his own people, possess his own mission stations, conserve the wealth accruing from all sources, if possible, for the commonwealth and enlightenment of the people and the glory of God.

Let Africa, which has so long been "last" take her rank amongst the first races of the earth by putting aside the curse of individual aggrandizement of labour for the greatest good of the whole African race, rather than the special enrichment of the favored and selfish few. Many may be able to invest money which they can not afford to give, and such investments may come to play an important part.

[39] Very much can be accomplished on semi-commercial lines of operation, care being taken in the selection of agents and officials of an established Christians character.

The writer would therefore suggest, as an auxiliary to further development, the formation of an

African Development Society[85]

on the basis defined in clause 14 of the objects of the Union, namely:
1. The shares not to be transferable without the directors' consent.
2. The shareholders to receive a moderate rate of interest only.
3. The shareholders liability to be limited.
4. The surplus property to become the property of the Union for the objects laid down.
   The capital suggested in the first instance is $250,000 in 50,000 $5 shares, with power to increase as may be found necessary.

---

[85] 1st ed has African Land and Transport Company as the title of this section.

AFRICA FOR THE AFRICAN.

Such a company would give scope to the capital and energies of those accustomed to business operations as well as afford a safe investment for part of the savings of the people, and at the same time become a benefit to both the Afro-American and the African native.

As before named, one English company named The British South African Chartered Company which has not been formed above seven years lays claim to a piece of Africa about half the size of Europe, said to be 500,000 square miles in extent. Another but, older company named the Royal Niger Company, claims a slice of Africa measuring about 750,000[86] square miles. This latter makes great wealth out of the palm oil produced in great quantities within its borders.

The culture of coffee, cotton, corn, oil plants, sugar, fiber, etc. would produce substantial returns in proper hands.

Maize, or Indian corn, grows very abundantly, but as the native only grows it (in B.C. Africa) for his own and family's use, not understanding commerce with other parts, the great demand at the large mining centres in the South is badly supplied and the prices are high - so much so that shiploads have of late been coming from America.

A special settlement should be formed for cotton growing, the country and climate being extremely favorable, but so far attention is centered upon the coffee plant in the high country adjacent to the Zambesi and Shire rivers. This is one of the few coffee growing countries free from the "leaf" disease so prevalent elsewhere.[87]

It should be one of the first objects of this Company to enter largely into or possess the traffic of the vast country opened out by the rivers named, together with the lakes, Nyassa, Tanganyika, Bangevolo[88] and

---

[86] 1st ed has 500,000.
[87] The last sentence was added in the second edition.
[88] Lake Bangweulu in Northeastern Zambia.

AFRICA FOR THE AFRICAN.

eventually by another route, the great lakes Victoria Nyassa and Albert Nyassa.

A student of Africa's development is struck by the immense power for good or evil that large companies come to wield. Taken as a rule, [40] and the exceptions are very few, they are tremendous agents of an anti missionary character. Their agents or employees are generally of a god-less character, or become so as the restraints of civilization are absent. Their immorality, i.e. of the majority of these employees, is notorious, and of too[89] flagrant a character to define[90].

This, therefore needs combatting on its own ground. Public money loaned out to make money can as well be employed by Christian men, living Christian lives, working with the natives in a Christian spirit and for distinctly Christian ends, protecting and encouraging, in place of driving, cursing and oppressing the people; as upon an anti-religious or non-religious basis. From personal knowledge and contact the writer can testify that such companies and their agents are too often great and efficient missionary societies of Satan. The very moral atmosphere of Africa is poisoned with such, until, in certain parts "Company men" has become to be the Natives' designation of all Europeans of a non Christian bearing.

Providing the management be fairly good and the articles of the Company afford liberal scope for expansion, and the agents be selected with care, such a Company as that now urged upon the Negro friends may accomplish[91] a preparatory work for the African race of great subsequent value.

As a beginning, the following programme is suggested:

---

[89] 1st ed has "two".
[90] 1st ed has "to write about" instead of "to define".
[91] 1st ed has "to accomplish".

AFRICA FOR THE AFRICAN.

A. The planting of 1000 Acres of Coffee at a cost of 8 pounds per acre from seed plant, ... £8,000. $40,000.00

B. The planting of 1,000 Acres of Cotton or Sugar at a cost of 5 pounds per acre from seed to fruit, ... 5,000.   25,000.00

C. The establishment of a River Transport Service, see Schedule F,[92] 12,000.   60,000.00

D. The investment in land in British territory at 2-6 per acre,... 1,000.   5,000.00

E. The investment in Native land outside the British sphere at 1 or 2 cents per acre, ... 14,000.   70,000.00

                                                                             40,000. $200,000.00

Reserve margin,   10,000. $50,000.00

For working Capital and Trading purposes,   £50,000. $250,000.00

[41] The question arises; "And what prospect[93] is there of this capital being safely and profitably engaged?" What is the ultimate return?

After the Company's operations are got into fair working order, the writer considers it a probable thing, and judging from what is now being done, that after paying the shareholders for the use of their capital a sum ranging from twenty to thirty thousand pounds or from one-hundred thousand dollars to one-hundred and fifty thousand dollars may be earned for the African Christian Union. (See schedule following:)

---

[92] 1st ed does not tell the reader to which schedule to refer.
[93] 1st ed has "profit".

AFRICA FOR THE AFRICAN.

Schedule E.

[Relating to the Proposed "African Development Society"]

	POUNDS	DOLLARS
To profit on Section A. 1000 acres of coffee at 15 pounds per acre [See Schedule B]	15,000.	75,000
To Same on Section B, viz: 1000 Acres of Cotton or Sugar at to pounds net per acre	10,000.	50,000
To Same on Section C, viz: River Transport Services, [See Schedule F]	6,450.	32,250
To Same on[94] sales of land in small sections to Negro or Native purchasers	500.	2,500
To Same on General trading Oil, Nuts, Maize, Rice, Rubber, etc., etc.	3,000.	15,000
	34,950	174,750
Less Home Office Expenses and Propaganda,	1,000	
Interest to Share-holders 5 per cent on £50,000[95]	2,500	
	£3,500 OR	$17,500
Leaving as the estimated net profit for the African Christian Union,	£31,450.	$157,250

---

[94] 1st ed has "Section D and E" inserted here.
[95] 1st ed mistakenly has £2500.

AFRICA FOR THE AFRICAN.

THE AUTHOR'S APOLOGY

[42] At the outset the writer promised some sort of "raison d'etre" for the publication of the foregoing pamphlet.

This necessitates a departure from the convenient third person to the distasteful first person singular and involves a review of the past which in many respects is a little objectionable. Yet since it may furnish some necessary clue to the somewhat egotistical stand the writer has found himself constrained to adopt in the attempt to acquire for the African his just rights it is hoped that the reader's clemency will expand to the occasion. For many reasons the simpler and more congenial course of "forgetting those things which are behind"[96] would have been preferred, but in order that the "roots" (as the natives say) of the project may be laid bare the following is volunteered.

I am an Englishman of the Midland Counties, of humble parentage. In 1877 I emigrated to Australia where I conducted farming and business operations passing through the usual vicissitudes incident to Colonial life. On the morning of the 26th day of February, 1886, my 35th birthday, came the turning point[97] in my life and the change which ultimates in the projects stated under the preceding pages headed "Africa for the Africans."

It came in this manner. My dear son, John Edward (now buried in Nyassaland)[98] came at daybreak to wish me a loving birthday greeting bringing with him a card on which he had written the text:

---

[96] See Philippians 3:14.
[97] 1st edition has "burning point".
[98] 1st ed has "up the Zambesi river" in place of Nyassaland.

AFRICA FOR THE AFRICAN.

Acknowledge Him in all thy ways and He will direct thy path.[99]

I looked into the boy's eyes; what did he mean? Did he know that I only professed to serve God and that my life was really utterly selfish? Had he chosen this as a rebuke? So I asked "How came you to choose these words my son?" The boy's answer and features convinced me that he believed me to be a genuine Christian, for he said "because it is a favorite text of yours, father, and you often give it to me to write." I was perplexed and confounded. What! was my own son, my only son, to become a witness against me at the day of judgment? This foreshadowing seemed to say so.

I could go out to face the world no more on the old self-seeking, God-dishonoring lines. I locked myself in a room alone with God, and did not, nay, could not, come out until relief and new purpose was found in the vow to do, or try to do, anything, or go anywhere that He would clearly show to be His will.

This vow by a series of events led me to devote the efforts of some years to the atheists and skeptics of Melbourne, Australia[100] conducting comfortable and profitable business operations at the same time. To the leader of those people, one Joseph Symes, I owe much. This man in response to the various replies to his many lectures, laid bare to me, in a new and startling way, the demands and responsibilities of Christ's gospel upon those accepting it.

He would ask who valued Christ's advice as much as their wealth? Who heeded His words "Sell all thou hast, give to the poor, come, follow me, and thou shalt have treasure in heaven."[101]

[43] Where were the followers of Christ who believed this to be a wise procedure? They were conspicuously absent. "When are you going to

---

[99] See Proverbs 3:6.
[100] 1st ed does not have Australia.
[101] See Matthew 19:21.

AFRICA FOR THE AFRICAN.

take His advice and when is the sale going to be, Mr. Booth;" he would triumphantly ask. This then was to me God's way of "showing" me the path to be taken.

On May 1st, 1891, this sale took place and my business career, for individual purposes, closed. Two journeys to England followed, to visit various Missionary Societies and offer my life services for any work in any part of the world, only to learn that "no aged need apply." The necessity of obeying the Lord's command "go ye" remained; and the painful fact was revealed[102] that whilst half a world was waiting for its gospel birthright the artificial standards of Missionary organizations excluded workers willing to labor for their own support and the[103] work's extension. The need for a more expansive basis freed from the remnants of ecclesiastical paraphernalia and demonstrating[104] the right and ability of Christ's representative to both support himself and minister to the needs of the work by a righteous and vigorous use of his wealth producing knowledge, either on union or sectarian lines, became thus apparent.[105]

The oversight of leaving the direct resources of God's rich earth to "the children of this world" whilst the extension of Missionary operations languished and their respective boards appealed vainly, though with vigor, for enlarged revenues, seemed obvious; and the necessity of attempting a basis commensurate with the ultimate super-structure[106] to be reared, viz: the gospel for "all people" seemed imperative.

These views were industriously pressed upon various secretaries persons interested in Missions, to all appearance fruitlessly; for no link of

---

[102] 1st ed has "reverted" instead of "revealed".
[103] 1st ed does not have "the".
[104] 1st ed has "demonstration".
[105] "Union" alludes to the interdenominational missions, while "sectarian" means denominational.
[106] 1st ed has "superb structure".

AFRICA FOR THE AFRICAN.

cooperation was formed; and heartsick of conferring with flesh and blood I quitted London in January 1892 for Africa, that continent presenting the most needy field in my judgment. On February 7th I reached Capetown, thence made my way into the interior.[107]

The solution to the great Mission problem appeared to have been first struck by Carey,[108] emphasized by Livingstone[109] and groped for by MacRay[110] in the principle "Make Missions self-supporting and self-propagating."

After some months' careful search for favorable conditions, suitable field and fairly safe source of revenue, the locality chosen as a centre affording ample future radiating scope, was the hill country of the Shire Highlands, B.C. Africa. Here on August 11th, 1892[111], I and my

---

[107]"thence..." did not appear in the 1st ed..
[108]William Carey (1761-1834) founded the Baptist Missionary Society in 1792, and thereafter served as a missionary in India. In his *Enquiry into the Obligation of Christians to use Means for the Conversion of the Heathens*, (Leicester: 1792), Carey wrote:
> In most countries it would be necessary for them to cultivate a little spot of ground just for their support, which would be a resource to them, whenever their supplies failed. Not to mention the advantages they would reap from each others company, it would take off the enormous expence which has always attended undertakings of this kind, the first expence being the whole .... so small a number would, upon receiving the first crop, maintain themselves. (p. 74).

[109]Livingstone believed that a combination of Christianity and commerce would bring an end to the save trade and "civilize" Africa. See note 41 on page 46.
[110]This seems to be a mispelling of Mackay, pioneer missionary to Uganda. Before going to Uganda with the Church Missionary Society, Mackay felt called to minister to the people of Madagascar as an "engineering missionary". "He wanted to go ... to teach the natives to build roads, bridges, railways, to work mines, and to learn to use various kinds of machinery, and so to help them become more useful Christians." Sophia Lyon Fahs, *Uganda's White Man of Work: A Story of Alexander M. Mackay*. (New York: Young People's Missionary Movement, 1907), 28.
[111]1st edition has 1892, without a specific date.

AFRICA FOR THE AFRICAN.

little daughter[112] (of 9 years) arrived, my son having stayed for a year's educational help in London.[113]

It was my purpose to have got at least fifty miles from any existing Mission station, but man proposes and God disposes. His disposition of events, completely locked me up by sickness and failure of resources to the vicinity of the Blantyre Mission[114] and that neighborhood (about 5 miles away) became the theatre of the infant effort, not as a recognized Mission, but as an individual matter. Naturally enough this nondescript effort taking to itself such a locality for its experimental home, excited indignation near and far, but in faith that the wisdom of God would in due time manifest the purpose of His choice, and evolve good[115] from seeming error, the stand was quietly[116] maintained and appeals for aid sent forth. Like flowers that bear hidden fragrance till they ripen, the bud period had some bitter stages.

A dear Wesleyan friend, by name Edward Mangin, who followed from Melbourne, Australia, died of fever on the 14th day and was buried on August 26th in the little graveyard at the Blantyre Mission. His grave was made side by side with one who had died in the April previous and who strange to say had come with the same purpose in his heart, viz: to become a self-supporting missionary. It is related by one who ridiculed his puny [44] effort, that before he died, being asked "what would now become of his self-supporting Mission?" that he gave the "stock reply" "the Lord will provide." In our coming to the same spot

---

[112] Booth's daughter, Emily Booth Langworthy, later described her life in Nyasaland in *This Africa was Mine*, (Stirling Tract Enterprises, 1950).
[113] Edward Booth had joined the East London Training Institute of Fanny and Grattan Guinness for missionary training.
[114] The Church of Scotland mission founded in memory of David Livingstone. For a history of the mission, see Andrew C. Ross, *Blantyre Mission and the Making of Modern Malawi*, (Blantyre: CLAIM, 1996).
[115] 1st ed has "make good" instead of "evolve good".
[116] 1st ed has "quickly".

and one of us falling, to lie by his side, I saw God's response to this brother's faith. "Humphrey Henchman" was the name of this little known but faithful pioneer. The need of making a very solemn stand was thus impressed upon me. On August 20th my little daughter was so low with fever that hourly I expected her death. For several months, from repeated attacks of fever she seemed to hang between life and death and I had but little suitable food for her weak state. The few Europeans who occasionally called at the hut we dwelt in, vigorously urged "go back, go back," looking upon me as little less than a criminal for remaining; but the fact was I could not read anything of a "go back" nature in my Lord's words, not even permission to "look back." If as these friends stated the price of our staying was my child's life and my own then let the price be paid, so long as He declared[117] "He that loseth his life for my sake shall find it."[118] Neither life, however, was called for. At this juncture resources which had been left in reserve to cover a fair period, utterly failed, owing to Australian[119] bank closures. Now came the test how far the hand of God would provide. I had sent letters and a plan of the proposed Industrial Mission far and wide in a dozen different directions. Would any strike root? This lay with God. It was for me to go forward to the end and see what His power would bring forth.

Jewelery and all spare clothing and some provisions were sold to acquire and clear land, purchase and plant seed and build a decent dwelling place. Seeds sufficient for 100 acres of coffee were carefully planted, but only plants enough for 20 acres were obtained; these were subsequently divided in two equal parts and given to the two missions which presently grew out of the appeals.

---

[117] 1st ed has "declare".
[118] **Matthew 16:23 and parallel verses.**
[119] **1st ed has "desperation" with no reference to Australia.**

AFRICA FOR THE AFRICAN.

On November 18th, 1892[120] came the first response by Mr. Caldwell of London; out of this came to be formed the present Zambesi Industrial Mission. In December there came responses from Australia which ultimately issued in the Nyassa Industrial Mission.

By April 1893 some thirty-five thousand acres of land in some nine or ten plots had been secured and by the ever willing and very cheerful aid of the natives some three-quarters of a million coffee plants were reared and several houses built by the time European helpers began freely to arrive.

Strange to say these early days of lone working with the natives was the charming period to which memory goes back with unblemished satisfaction. It is this period that inspires me with gratitude and a profound belief in the grand possibilities of the Central African if he can be saved from the Anglo-Saxon's mad rush for territory and gold, heedlessly trampling under foot all rights of black men that are inconvenient to him and his heartless methods.

During this luminous period the cantankerous spirit which so often takes root in a company of Europeans with differing grades of "good will" to the African, was unknown. The many and beautiful acts of kindness to myself and little child I shall never forget. Some kindness was shown my child by the Missionaries of Blantyre and very marked facilities and even kindly favor was accorded to the Mission programme by the then consul general, now Sir H.H. Johnston, but the surprising interest and aid of the natives themselves remains yet a marvel to me. Whole chapters and many of them would be needed to relate the many developments in this direction which surprised me.

They labored for calico value 2 & 6[121] (60 cents) per month. As the work progressed there were four or five hundred workers from four or

---

[120] 1st ed has "On November the 18th", with no mention of the year.
[121] 1st ed has 46 instead of 2 & 6.

AFRICA FOR THE AFRICAN.

five tribes. No work seemed to be a task to these friends. Forest clearing, timber sawing, [45] road and brick making,[122] building, nursery gardening, load carrying, &c.[123] To go from one set to another and direct or inspect their work was to meet with cheerful greetings and trustful willing faces anxious to please and grateful for a pleasant or encouraging word. I have been accustomed to direct farm and other hired labor for many years, but it has never been my fortune to find work done with such delightsome willingness and with such a spirit of brotherhood prevailing. But the scene changed[124] and tests of a new character overtook the work. Many helpers poured into the field; some thirty and more thousands of pounds were given by the public; my policy to the natives was severely challenged as too liberal by my co-workers.[125] I took this as indicating[126] that the Lord had need of me for other work and so retired in the close of 1894, there being many workers and supporters glad to carry on the work on the level they approved.[127]

I believed it to be my duty to make a further effort to establish a similar organization in connection with the Baptist friends. I therefore visited this body in England, Scotland and in America, the Negro Baptists. The English responded by taking up and carrying through[128] the Nyassa Industrial Mission and the Scotch formed the Baptist Industrial Mission of Scotland. The Negro friends gave me a kindly hearing,

---

[122] 1st ed lists these tasks separately as "road making, brick making...".
[123] "&c." was added in the second edition.
[124] 1st ed has "changes".
[125] 2nd ed adds "by my co-workers", who are not clearly identified. Booth may be refering to missionaries of the Zambezi Industrial Mission, see Langworthy, *The Life of Joseph Booth*, 67-68. The Presbyterian missionaries of Blantyre Mission also complained that Booth paid unnecessarily high wages which attracted their adherents to his missions where they would receive more pay (ibid. p. 56).
[126] 1st ed has "indication".
[127] "on the level they approved" does not appear in the 1st ed.
[128] "through" does not appear in the 1st ed.

AFRICA FOR THE AFRICAN.

but did not commence operations. The need of a separate transport agency to carry supplies, produce and Mission workers was felt and after considerable effort a Missionary Transport Company pledged to give its profits to Industrial Missionary work was floated and left in working order in other hands.

This brief period of five years has, therefore, been a kind of educational or novitiate period. I was wishful to see the[129] root principle of self-support and self-extension worked out by other hands and observe the results.

These are satisfactory from the revenue producing standpoint;[130] the failure is in another direction; it lies in the difficulty of fully bridging the gulf between the European and the native.

The policy advocated by me and the programme for which the public support was originally solicited was that the promising Native Christians should be trained and fitted to take charge of stations *themselves* under European oversight; that they should be admitted when qualified, to hold equal positions and be entitled to take charge of their own stations on parallel lines with the European missionary and that a Training Institute should be provided and a fair opportunity afforded the Native to acquire the needed knowledge. So far this important aspect of the work has been allowed to lapse. The Cause of this lower level being struck and the Native Christian not being admitted to, or qualified for parity of position, seems to be the fact that the majority of Missionaries do not approve that policy and so do not practise it. The Native is quick to note the early statements of the Missionary that he has come "to help" the African. He believes and plods on. By and

---

[129] "the" does not appear in the 1st ed.
[130] Until the terrible coffee blight in 1929, both the Zambesi and the Nyassa Industrial Missions were largely self-supporting. See *The Zambezi Industrial Mission* (31 March 1930).

AFRICA FOR THE AFRICAN.

bye he sees goodly[131] houses, with snug surroundings and manifold conveniences, but almost, likely enough altogether, enjoyed by Europeans, whilst he gets a few crumbs of aid, generally not so much as he would from worldly employers, and he begins to ask "is this help"? Have they not come to help themselves? This feature of the apparent inability of so many Christians to give the African Christian a full open handed opportunity to reach the same level as himself; his seemingly ingrained conviction, that the African is inherently inferior in capacity needs determinately rooting out. It is the root of all the wrong doing that has been heaped on the whole African race. Even Missionaries, many of them need teaching that the African is inferior in opportunity only and he is expressly commanded to give him the same measure of opportunity which he would desire for himself. It is this difficult feature in the majority of Christians that has [46] produced the present effort to get the educated Christian black man to his needy black brother. He at any rate cannot hold[132] the deadly belief in the black man's born inferiority.

I would like to remark in passing that in this matter of liberally qualifying the approved Native Christian for holding responsible positions and replacing the European workers, as they retire with Native successors, the Blantyre Mission of the Church of Scotland sets an admirable example, and has shown a truly generous Christian spirit.[133]

In South Africa, indeed I venture to say in all Africa, the Lovedale Native Institution[134] is the most liberal in the range of knowledge imparted to the Native. Here though the pupil is wisely made to contribute

---

[131] 1st ed has "good by" here.
[132] 1st ed has "cannot note".
[133] See Andrew Ross, *Blantyre Mission and the Making of Modern Malawi*, (Blantyre: CLAIM, 1996), especially chapters 6 and 7 describing D.C. Scott and Alexander Hetherwick as leaders of the mission and their relations with the African deacons in their church.
[134] Lovedale in South Africa, founded in 1841 by the Free Church of Scotland as an Industrial Mission, it provided a model for the Overton Institution of Livingstonia Mission.

AFRICA FOR THE AFRICAN.

towards his own support and so taught the value of his instruction, he may attain full access to the stores of knowledge the English language affords him the key to. The South African Colonist desires to keep English from the Native and so lock him up within the limited range of his own language and to this desire most Missions have bowed either to suit the spirit of the times or to avoid the trouble involved. The favourite excuse is that they are sent to "preach" not to educate.

Being impressed greatly with the need of sympathetic African educated Christian teachers for the receptive Central African and having been unsuccessful in my appeal to the Negroes of America I waited an opportunity to visit South Africa and so discover what suitable material there was amongst the converts of the different Missions for the "Regions beyond" of Central Africa.[135] An opportunity was providentially afforded, and the programme as defined by the 21 objects of the then proposed "African Christian Union" was printed in English, Zulu and the native tongue of Cape Colony; by means of reproduction in the public press and the Native Newspaper *Jendo* the proposal became well known over a wide area, inclusive of the Dutch speaking states. I discovered there was a wealth of suitable Native Christian converts but my sojourn was too brief (owing to other preengagements) to bring the visit to any immediate and practical issue. A wonderful interest was aroused, but the underlying and insurmountable difficulty to the majority was the fact that such proposals emanated from an European.

Any such proposals from such[136] a source must have some hidden trap that would ultimately be sprung upon them[137]; some cleverly hidden poison wrapped up in sweet words and luring suggestions. There was no living European who could be absolutely trusted where the African's rights were concerned. Astonishing to relate the greater the schol-

---

[135] 1st ed has "to the 'Regions Beyond' of Central Africa"
[136] "such" does not appear in the first edition.
[137] "them" does not appear in the first edition.

AFRICA FOR THE AFRICAN.

ars, the greater the distrust, doubtless owing to their wider vision of the wrongs sustained by their people as contrasted with the fuller knowledge of God's requirements. This vision of the manifold charges written in the hearts of this great and increasing cloud of African witnesses and ascending to God night and day against the iniquities of my own race is the most saddening and oppressive experience of my life.

In the record of European and African contact during the past half century inclusive of the present time only one European publicly known by the Natives has received their full confidence and absolute trust, that man they named

"SO-BANTU"

He now lies buried with that name on his tombstone in the church of Pietermaritzburg, Natal.[138]

It seems to me therefore that the greatest hindrance to the progress of God's work in Africa is the painful fact that as the Native gets to know us Europeans and our little ways he calmly concludes we are a nation of robbers, [47] nothing less. He could tolerate the robbery better if we did not preach up honesty so persistently.

Here is a sample of what I mean.

Thirty years ago the first white man visited British Central Africa, by name David Livingstone. His words were of peace and brotherhood and his memory was treasured.

Fifteen years ago others followed, they were Missionaries; their words also were sweet, they speak of "peace and good will". They asked a place to settle and teach. The Ajawa Chief Kapeni[139] referred to by

---

[138]The place of burial was blank in the 1st ed.
[139]Kapeni, a Yao chief in the Blantyre area, maintained a close relationship with the Blantyre Missionaries throughout his reign. D.C. Scott for example

AFRICA FOR THE AFRICAN.

Livingstone (see *Zambesi and its tributaries*)[140] received them and gave them all the land they wished (a square mile in extent). Warning was sent to Kapeni by other chieftains, by name Kawinga[141], McKanda[142], and Livonde[143] living a little further inland. They said "Do not receive the white men. We have travelled to the coast and seen their ways. Others will follow them and when they are strong enough will take your land and tax you if you stay there; send them away; if they will not go, kill them."

Kapeni asked the Missionaries "was this so? Would these things follow if he receive them?" They said "No, the British did not 'do as the Portuguese did', whom his friends had seen."

Then Kapeni sent the word to his friends what the white teachers had answered and said he believed them and should not send them away, their words were only of peace.

The reply came "let them not come further, if they come into our land they must die" and still urged Kapeni to send them away. His final reply to them was, (and they were of the same Ajawa tribe as himself) "If they wished the white teachers sent away or killed, they must first fight with and conquer him. While he lived he should protect them."

---

participated in Kapeni's *milandu*, the traditional courts. See A.C. Ross, *Blantyre Mission*, 69.
[140]David and Charles Livingstone, *Narrative of an Expedition to the Zambezi and Its Tributaries*, (London, 1865).
[141]Kawinga was chief in the area north of Zomba who was active in the slave trade. Andrew Ross, *Blantyre Mission*, 88, 98, 163.
[142]Mkanda was a Yao chief in the Mulanje area.
[143]Chief Liwonde had allowed the Universities' Mission to Central Africa to build a school in his village in 1888, but later his relations with Europeans soured. See W.P. Johnson, *My African Reminiscences*, (Westminister: UMCA, nd [1924]), 158-9, 205. Liwonde was deposed by the British in 1895, Eric Stokes, "Malawi Political Systems and the Introduction of Colonial Rule", in Eric Stokes; Richard Brown (eds.), *The Zambesian Past. Studies in Central African History*, (Manchester University Press, 1969), 353-375 [368].

AFRICA FOR THE AFRICAN.

Six years ago the British Government entered this country and undertook to "protect"[144] the people. Those chiefs are still living some in prison for defending their homes and some have fled beyond the British sphere, but their land is gone, their people are taxed and the three forts by name Fort Johnson[145], Fort Sharp[146] and Fort Liwonde on the Upper Shire now "protect" their country; from whom? Kapeni is now dead and his son bearing his name having withstood the aggression is a free man.

Take another instance; over four years ago the writer thankfully received a grant of 5 one thousand acre blocks of land from H.M. Consul General in the Angoni Country.

No[147] European was then residing in that land. The Natives were paid for the land chosen as they denied any right on the part of the British Consul to give their land away. In due[148] time 9 or 10 Missionaries were placed at those stations. The Chief of the country Gomani[149], had often been urged by distant chiefs to drive the Missionaries out of his land but since they had bought the land in a satisfactory manner he would not do so, but sent his people to work at the plantations attached to these stations and for carrying their loads. Like most other chiefs he dealt more or less in slaves and doubtless needed to be warned and stopped by proper means.

An expedition was sent, the chief and some of his leading men killed, the whole of the country was appropriated and the subject people who

---

[144] Quotation marks were added in the second edition.
[145] Fort Johnston, named after Sir Harry Johnston, is now Mangochi.
[146] Fort Sharpe was named after Alfred Sharpe, who was governor of the British Central African Protectorate from 1891 to 1910. It was located in the vicinity of Chief Liwonde's town. Robert Boeder, *Alfred Sharpe of Nyasaland: Builder of Empire*, (Blantyre: Society of Malawi, 1981), 46.
[147] 1st ed incorrectly has "The European" instead of "No European".
[148] 1st ed has "one"
[149] 1st ed misspells the name as Gomain.

AFRICA FOR THE AFRICAN.

had done no wrong, were forthwith put under the hut tax. The price of the land in this country is now half a crown per acre. Curiously enough the Native troops used to secure this British victory were some of the Ajawa Natives formerly conquered and who feel themselves thus bound to obey their conquerors[150].

[48] Can we be satisfied with an extension of territory acquired in such a manner? Can a greater hindrance to a gospel of peace and good will be conceived?

Take yet another instance, showing the effect on the native mind.

An earnest Native Convert, by name John Chilembwe,[151] an Ajawa, recently narrated the following.

> I often preach in my native village, but the chief and many people will not hear now. One day after preaching my older brother came to me and said "you preach just now that God's message is to go to all people and tell a good message to them. How do you know?" I answered "because I can read it for myself both in the English tongue and in my own language. I have God's book." He said "but perhaps white men have altered God's book to suit themselves and so they preach peace to us. Perhaps God's book does not say this to white men; perhaps it

---

[150] 1st ed has "conqueror" (singular).
[151] John Chilembwe was Booth's house servant whom he educated and took to America in 1897 where Chilembwe attended seminary in Virginia. Chilembwe later returned to Malawi to establish the Providence Industrial Mission with backing from the African-American National Baptist Church. In 1915 he was killed after leading a nationalist Rising against the British. Though Booth was a pacifist and had no foreknowledge of the event, his relationship to Chilembwe lead him to be deported from both Lesotho and South Africa in 1915. For details on the Rising, see Shepperson and Price, *Independent African*, (Edinburgh University Press, 1958). For more on Booth's relationship with Chilembwe see Langworthy, *The Life of Joseph Booth*.

says to them go to all people, take their land; kill the people, I give you power.

If God's word said to them, what they preach to us, 'not to steal, not to kill,' would they not do it? I cannot receive the words which the white men have brought."

It is an easy thing to go with the flood and to soothe oneself with the reflection that the Missionary's instructions are simply to "preach the gospel" and leave these things to right themselves.

I however must make one, having been "shown" the wickedness of these proceedings to "try" in God's name and strength to stop them, in such way as He shall guide. I can afford to lay down life anytime or where in His service; but[152] I cannot afford to be a participator, by passiveness, in such stupendous and widespread wrongs as I perceive are being abundantly inflicted upon the African race.

> Hence this my appeal
> first, to the British Queen and Government
> second, to the British and American European Christians
> third and specially
> > to the Negroes of the United States and West Indies
>
> that "Africa for the African" be made a reality as far as each have the power to bring that about.

In conclusion, may I be allowed to say that, whilst this appeal is penned in full belief that spiritual weapons are finally more powerful than carnal it is well to remember the fact that although "God's mill grinds slowly" it grinds surely and very fine[153]. This was made manifest in His way of emancipating the American slave. What Britain had done with noble generosity the American States were reluctantly compelled to do by wading through a red sea of blood.

---

[152] 1st ed does not have "but", and instead has two separate sentences.
[153] "and very fine" does not appear in the 1st ed.

AFRICA FOR THE AFRICAN.

It remains for the Christians of Britain in this day, to consider, whether in the spirit of President Lincoln's solemn confession during the Nation's deadly struggle, we also shall be able to say, if the needs arises,

> if all the treasure that has been heaped up by the spoliation of the African has to be expended; and if every drop of African blood shed in the effort to appropriate his country, has to be blotted out by an equal expenditure of European blood just, and righteous, O God, are all thy judgments.[154]

As Britain set the example in times past in regard to her West Indian slaves may she now have the wisdom and courage to restore Africa to the African as far as her power extends.[155]

---

[154] Booth appears to have adapted Lincoln's Second Inaugural Address given March 4, 1865:
> Fondly do we hope, fervently do we pray, that this mighty scourge of war may speedily pass away. Yet, if God wills that it continue until all the wealth piled up by the bond-man's two hundred and fifty years of unrequited toil shall be sunk, and until every drop of blood drawn with the sword, as was said three thousand years ago, so it must be said, "The judgements of the Lord are true and righteous altogether."

Reprinted *Abraham Lincoln: Speeches and Writings 1859*-1865, (New York: Literary Classics of the United States, distributed by Viking Press, 1989), 687.

[155] "to restore Africa to the African as far as her power extends" does not appear in the 1st ed.

SCHEDULES.

[49]

Schedule A.

Objects of the Society:-[156]

1. To unite together in the name of Jesus Christ such persons as desire to see full justice done to the African race and are resolved to work towards and pray for the day when the African people shall become an African Christian Nation.
2. To provide capital to equip and develop Industrial Mission Stations worked by competent Native Christians or others of the African race; such stations to be placed on a self supporting and self propagating basis.
3. To steadfastly demand by Christian and lawful methods the equal recognition of the African and those having blood relationship, to the rights and privileges accorded to Europeans.
4. To call upon every man, woman and child of the African race, as far as may be practicable, to take part in the redemption of Africa during this generation, by gift, loan or personal services.
5. To specially call upon the Afro-American Christians, and those of the West Indies to join hearts and hands in the work either by coming in person to take active part or by generous, systematic contributions[157].
6. To solicit funds in Great Britain, America and Australia for the purpose of restoring at their own wish[158] carefully selected

---

[156]The wording of this differs from Booth's original 1896 version. For a full comparison of this version with the original, see Langworthy, *The Life of Joseph Booth*, 77-84.
[157]1st ed has "contribution" (singular).
[158]"at their own wish" does not appear in the first edition.

AFRICA FOR THE AFRICAN.

Christian Negro families, or adults of either sex, back to their fatherland in pursuance of the objects of the Union; and to organize an adequate propaganda to compass the work.

7. To apply such funds in equal parts to the founding of Industrial Mission centres and to the establishing of Christian Negro settlements.

9.[159] To firmly, judiciously and repeatedly place on record by voice and pen for the information of the uninformed, the great wrongs inflicted upon the African race in the past and in the present, and to urge upon those who wish to be clear of African blood in the day of God's judgments, to make restitution for the wrongs of the past and to withstand the appropriation of the African's land in the present.

10. To initiate, or develop the culture of Tea, Coffee, Cocoa, Sugar, etc., etc., and to establish profitable mining or other industries or manufactures.   [50]

11. To establish such transport agencies by land, river, lakes or ocean as shall give the African free access to the different parts of his great country and people, and to the general commerce of the world.

12. To engage qualified persons to train and teach African learners any department of Commercial, Engineering, nautical, professional or other necessary knowledge.

13. To mould and guide the labor of Africa's millions into channels that shall develop the vast God-given wealth of Africa for the uplifting and commonwealth of the people, rather than for the aggrandisement of a few already rich persons.

14. To promote the formation of Companies on a Christian basis devoted to special aspects of the work; whose liability shall be limited, whose shares shall not be transferrable without the

---

[159] There is no point 8 in either original edition.

society's consent: whose shareholders shall receive a moderate rate of interest only; whose profits shall permanently become the property of the Trustees of the African Christian Union, for the prosecution of the defined objects of the Union.

15. To petition the government of the United States of America to make a substantial monetary grant to each adult Afro-American desiring to be restored to African soil, as some recognition of the 250 years of unpaid slave labor and the violent abduction of millions of Africans from their native land.

16. To petition the British and other European governments holding or claiming African territory to generously restore the same to the African people or at the least to make adequate inalienable native reserve lands, such reserves to be convenient to the locality of the different tribes.

17. To petition the British and other European governments occupying portions of Africa to make substantial and free grants of land to expatriated Africans or their descendants desiring restoration to their fatherland, such grants to be made inalienable from the African race.

18. To provide for all representatives, officials, or agents of the Union and its auxiliaries, inclusive of the Companies it may promote modest, economical yet efficient and as far as may be, equable, maintenance, together with due provision for periods of sickness, incapacity, widow-hood or orphanage.

19. To print and publish literature in the interest of the African race and furnish periodical accounts of the transactions of the Society and its auxiliary agencies, the same to be certified by recognized auditors and to be open to the fullest scrutiny of the Union's supporters.   [51]

20. To vest all funds, properties, products, or other sources of income in the hands of Trustees, not less than seven in number, to be held in perpetuity in the distinct interest of the African race

AFRICA FOR THE AFRICAN.

and for the accomplishment of the objects herein set forth in 21 clauses.

21. Finally, to pursue steadily and unswervingly the policy:
"AFRICA FOR THE AFRICAN"
and look for and hasten by prayer and united effort the forming of a united.
AFRICAN CHRISTIAN NATION
By God's power and blessing and in His own time and way.

[Signed] JOSEPH BOOTH,
English Missionary.

Dated January 14th, 1897,

JOHN CHILEMBWE,
at Ajawa Christian Native.

Blantyre, Nyassaland, ALEXANDER DICKIE,
English Missionary.[160]

East Central Africa.

MORRISON MALINKA,
Native Christian Chipeta Tribe.[161]

---

[160] Alexander Dickie was a missionary of the Zambezi Industrial Mission. He was very devoted to African interests and supported Booth by providing finances enabling Booth and Chilembwe to travel to the United States. Langworthy, *The Life of Joseph Booth*, 84.

[161] Malinka was probably one of the Booth's earliest converts; he was a longtime associate of Booth in the Zambezi Industrial Mission. Ibid., 64, 84.

AFRICA FOR THE AFRICAN.

Schedule B.

Designed to show the outlay necessary to establish an Industrial Mission Station on a self-propagating basis.

STAFF OF EACH STATION AT MATURITY,

Pastor, ... 1
Medical Man, ... 1
Schoolmaster, ... 1
Planter and 2 Practical Assistants, ... 3
On Furlough, ... <u>2</u>

                          Total 8

INDUSTRY PLANTATION WORK-FIRST YEAR-COFFEE.

To Capital to be supplied as needed   [$10,000][162] £2,000

COFFEE COCOA, TEA, &C. - FIRST YEAR - OUTLAY.

By	Land, 1,000 acres at 2s. 6d,	£125
"	Sundry fees,	25
"	Fares and outfit of two artisan workers, carpenter and nurseryman,	150
"	Provisions for two, one year, at £50 each (see note b.)[163]	100
"	Tools, etc.,	100
"	Seeds, £25, Sundries, £25,	50
"	Wages of natives,	250

                        £660 or $3,300[164]

---

[162] All dollar equivalents following this one on this schedule were added in the second edition.
[163] 1st ed incorrectly had £30.

AFRICA FOR THE AFRICAN.

SECOND YEAR

By	Fares and outfits of two further workers	£150
"	Provisions for four,	200
"	Seeds, tools, etc	100
"	Natives' wages,	250
	£700 or $3,500	

THIRD YEAR

By	Provisions for four,	£200
"	Natives' wages,	250
"	Sundries,	50
	£500 or $2,500	

$10,000 or £2,000

FOURTH YEAR

To yield 200 acres at 5 cwt., per acre, 50 tons at £90			£4,500
By	fares for outfit of four further workers @ £50 each	£200	
"	Provisions for six @ £50 each	300	
"	Furlough for two @ £150 each,	300	
"	Tools etc, further native wages	600	
"	Export charges on 50 tons @ £8	400	
		£1,800	
"	Capital for duplicate station,........................£2,000		
"	Surplus to reserve fund,..................... 700	2,700	
	$22,000 or £4,500	£4,500	

---

[164] Booth's addition is incorrect. Figures should be £800 and $4000.

AFRICA FOR THE AFRICAN.

FIFTH YEAR

To yield 300 acres at 5 cwt. per acre, 75 tons @ £90			£6,750
By	Provision for six persons @ £30 each,	300	
"	Furlough for two @ £30 each,	300	
"	Sundries,	100	
"	Wages to natives,	700	
"	Export charges on 75 tons @ £8 per ton,	600	
		£2,000	
"	Capital for duplicate station, ... £2,750		
"	Surplus to restore food, ... 2,750		
"	Credit balance, ... $22,850 or 4,750	£4,750	
			£6,750 £6,750

SEVENTH YEAR.

[Station now attains maturity.]

To yield 500 acres at 5 cwt. per acre, 125 tons @ 90			£10,800
By	provision of 8 persons at 50,	400	
"	Furlough for two	300	
"	Sundries	100	
"	Natives' wages	800	
"	Export charges, freight etc on 125 tons at £8	1,000	
		£2,600	
"	Capital for duplication to station $2,000		
"	Surplus to reserve fund 6,200		
"	Credit balance £8,200	8,200	
			£10,800 £10,800

AFRICA FOR THE AFRICAN.

NOTES.

a. The figure of 5 cwt.[165] per acre is arrived at thus: There are 1,500 per acre, planted as they are 5 ft. by 5 ft. apart. The yield is frequently 1s. and over per plant, but 6d. per plant is a common average, yet the estimate is based on less than[166] 4d. per plant and around for safety. Again[167] by weight per acre, the yield varies from 6 to 10 cwt. per acre; this is realizing in London and South Africa markets, 84s. to 112s. per cwt. Natal growers consider 10 cwt. per acre a moderate yield.

b. The figure £50 yearly for maintenance may appear small, but it must be remembered that each station can readily produce its own vegetables, poultry, sheep and goats, and often cattle.

c. It is not[168] intended to plant more than 500 acres each 1,000 plantation, so as to reserve 250 acres for native use, and 250 acres for buildings, gardens, orchard, playground, roads, etc.

d. No serious fear need be entertained of Africa over-stocking the world's markets, since she (Africa) is rapidly growing a larger consumer than producer.

e. A furlough every fourth year is provided for in view of the trying nature of the African Industrial work.

---

[165] 1st edition has £25.
[166] "less than" was added in second edition.
[167] 1st ed has "then" after "Again".
[168] "not" was added in second edition

AFRICA FOR THE AFRICAN.

Schedule C

Relating to Pamphlet, "Africa for the African."

Designed to show the progressive power of a mission station on a self-propagating basis, each station duplicating itself yearly after the fourth year and each offshoot maintaining the same ratio of progression:-

Year	
1,	1 station,
2	do.
3	do.
4	do.
5	1 Duplicate Station.
6	1
7	1
8	1
9	2
10	3
11	4
12	5
13	7
14	10
15	14
16	19
17	26
18	36
19	50
20	69
21	95
	344 Sub-stations
	1 Parent do.
Total Product	345

AFRICA FOR THE AFRICAN.

The capital sum of £7,500,000, should that come to be available over the ten year's period, as suggested would furnish 3,750 such centres, at a cost of £2,000 each; these duplicating on the scale shown above give the following arithmetical result; 3750 x 345= 1,283,750[169], which reduced fifty per cent to cover contingencies, yields a total of 646,375 such centres as a not impossible result, or one to each 400 persons, reaching 257 millions in number.

Schedule D.

Designed to show the possible power of the proposed Negro Christian Settlement programme.

Basis of settlement:

A. Ten families to form a settlement.
B. The whole to be under a superintendent appointed by the Union.
C. The area of land to be 2,000 acres for each settlement.
D. Each family to be allotted 200 acres.
E. 3,000 pounds capital to be available for the whole.
F. During the first seven years modest maintenance to be provided and such allowance further as the executive considers to be merited.
G. After seven years, the 200 acre estate with plantation and all appliances to become the absolute property of the settler.

---

[169]Actual figure should be 1,293,750, half of which is 686,475.

AFRICA FOR THE AFRICAN.

PRODUCE: Coffee, Tea, Cocoa, Corn, Cotton, Sugar, etc.
Approximate ESTIMATE PER SETTLEMENT.

American		English
£1,200	Outlay-By Land, 2000 acres at 2s. 6d	£250
150	" Survey fees	£30
	" Fares of ten families (say thirty Persons) at 30 pounds each*	£900
4,500	" Provisions and seed for three years beside the food produced	600
750	" Tools and sundries	150
750	" Superintendents' extra allowance of 50 pounds yearly	150
3,000	" Natives' extra labor 200 pounds yearly	600
$13,350		2,680
1,600	Margin for contingencies	320
$14,950		£3,000

N.B. Any crops produced and sold during the first three years are treated as a further margin for safety.

To be in cultivation and to profit.

by the 4th year, averaging £10 per acre net profit .. £4,000 or 20,000
" " 5th " ....6,000 " 30,000
" " 6th " ....8,000 " 40,000
" " 7th "1000 ....10,000 " 50,000
      Total estimate, net profit ...... £28,000 " 140,000

Capital required from each settlement to transplant
provided for a five-fold party; viz, five stations
at £3000 each .... 15,000 or 75,000
thus leaving a possible margin for contingencies of. £13,000 or $65,000

AFRICA FOR THE AFRICAN.

Assuming that the process proves practicable during a period of 28 years, the power of each parent station would be thus, the ratio of multiplication being five-fold:

1st year,	10	families
7th "	50	"
14th "	250	"
21st "	1250	"
28th "	6250	"

so that each settlement would have a possible, even probable, power of dealing with 6250 families and placing them in a position of competency and in possession of an estate of 200 acres with 100 acres developed and yielding a substantial income. Beyond this, each Christian settlement should be an effectual object lesson and centre of gospel light.

But should the assumed capital of 7½ million pounds be available over the ten years' period, the number of parent settlements thus provided for would be 2,500. We have, therefore, to multiply the figures of 6,250 families by the 2,500 stations, when the product becomes 15,625,000, as the number of families for whom, it is not impossible, provision could be made.

When, therefore, the fund thus created has done its work, it should become available for such approved African natives as the executive may deem needy and worthy of such aid.

[For schedule E, see page 72.]

Schedule F.

[Relating to the River Transport Service]

Note 1.   A Service of this nature in the hands of and controlled by staunch friends of the African is indispensable to the proposals set forth in "Africa for the Africans" as regards East Central Africa[170].

Note 2.   It is hoped that ere long a direct line of Steamers from American to African ports will be established either as an extension of the African Development Society's operations or as a separate Africa American Line[171].

Note 3.   The small flotilla hereunder described must be looked upon as a beginning only and equal to but a small part of the rapidly growing traffic.

Note 4.   The sphere of operations would in the first year or two be confined to the country reachable by the Zambesi and Shire rivers for a distance of about 300 miles, both rivers being obstructed by "Falls," or rapids at that distance from the coast. For the Upper Rivers and Lakes further accommodation would be needed.

Note 5.   Average duration of Steamer journey up river, 8 days, and 4 days down; average duration by sailing barges 12 days up and 5 days down river.[172]

Flotilla: Stern wheel Steamer, 90 by 15 feet, 4 steel sailing house boats or barges.

Capacity of Steamer: First Class Passengers, 12; Second class Passengers, 15; Deck Passengers, 30; Cargo, 40 tons.

Capacity of Each Sailing Barge: First Class Passengers, 6: Second Class passengers, 6: Cargo 12 tons.

Present Rates for same journey, viz: Chindi, Zambesi to Blantyre or Tete. Passengers $12 ONE Class only; Goods 8 pounds per ton.

---

[170]"as regards East Central Africa" does not appear in the first ed..
[171]1st edition has "Afro-American Line".
[172]Second edition adds the words "river" after up, "and" after 8 days, "down" after 4 days. The first edition lists the average duration by sailing barges as 10 days up and 8 days down.

AFRICA FOR THE AFRICAN.

ESTIMATED OUTLAY.

3 plots of Land for depots with stores and agents' houses,	1500	7500
East Stern wheel Steamer	4500	22500
6 Sailing House barges at 450[173] each	2700	13500
Sundries	500	2500
	£9200.	46000
Margin for Working and Trading Capital[174]	2800.	14000
	£12000.	60000

ESTIMATE INCOME

	Eng.	U.S[175]
To 20 Trips yearly of 1 Steamer towing 2 barges at a profit of £335 per trip[176]		£6700

UP-RIVER

50 Tons Cargo at £6	300.	1500
8 Passengers at 10	80.	400
10 Second Class Passengers at £6	60.	300
20 Deck Passengers at £3	90.	450[177]

DOWN-RIVER

30 Tons Cargo at £3	90.	450
10 Passengers at £6	60.	300
10 Deck Passengers at £2	20.	100
	700.	£3500
Less Expenses (well known to the writer) are under one half, say	365.	1825
Net Profit per Trip	£335.	$1675

---

[173] 1st ed incorrectly has 460 here.
[174] 1st ed has "Docking Capital" in place of "Working and Trading Capital".
[175] Dollar equivalents were added in the second edition.
[176] "per trip" was added in second edition.
[177] Figures should be 60 and 300 for 20 deck passengers, or 90 and 450 for 30 passengers.

AFRICA FOR THE AFRICAN.

BARGE TRAFFIC

To 12 Trips of 4 Barges at $300 Net per Round trip, ... 3600

UP-RIVER

4 Barges - 40 Tons Cargo at £6 .... 240.	1200
10 Passengers at £8 .... 80.	400
40 Deck Passengers at £2 .... 80.	400

DOWN-RIVER

20 Tons Cargo at £3 .... 60.	300
10 Passengers at £5 .... 50.	250
to Deck Passengers at £1 to 10 shillings ..... 15.	75
	525.	2625
The expenses are about one-third, viz: £175, say .... 225.	1125
Net Profit per trip	£300.	1500

                                                                                                       10,300

DEDUCT-Repairs, Insurance etc, 25 per cent,
of 9000 pounds.. 2250.
Interest on 12000 pounds.. 600.
Allow further for contingencies or Reserve .... 1000.

                                                                                                       3850.

Net Profit available for the Africa Christian Union   £6450. or $32,250

Note-At present, 1897, the traffic on the Zambesi and Shire river finds full employment for 12 steamers and over 30 large boats at higher rates than the above named. - J.B.[178]

---

[178] Booth's final note was added in the second edition.

AFRICA FOR THE AFRICAN.

The following pages are reproductions of the unnumbered pages which were added to the second edition. The pictures on this page appear opposite p.16, the Assembly is opposite p. 17. Nursery and Brook are opposite p. 32, Coffee Plants and Christian's House opposite p. 33, Mitsidi House is opposite p. 49.   -The Editor

CLEARED FOREST- Ready for Planting.

MY SON'S GRAVE,
And Those of Three Fellow Labourers.

My dear boy, John Edward, from his 14th year till his death, headed his letters "Africa for Christ." He died in his 18th year from over-exhaustion on a difficult journey.

"And with the mourn, those Angel faces smile,
Which have loved long since, and lost awhile."

105

AN ASSEMBLY AT THE MISSION HOUSE.

NURSERY.

For Coffee Plant Seedlings - this is a clearing, shaded by the forest trees and near a stream of water where the seeds are planted in beds one hundred feet long and five feet wide, the seeds being about three inches apart in rows four inches apart, subsequently, the young plants are transplanted 9 inches apart.

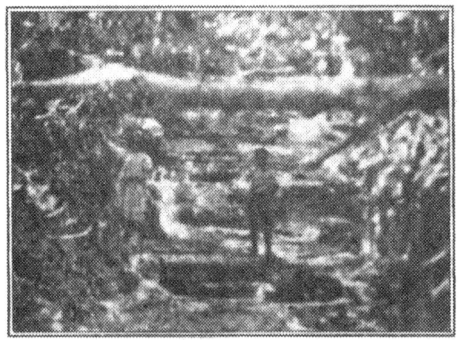

A BONNIE BROOK
On the Mitsidi Station.

YOUNG COFFEE PLANTS.

The particular plants shown in this picture have a history. The seeds were sown in September 1892 in faith, for there were no human supporters and my own money was finished, hence it became necessary to sell all spare clothing, etc. to pay Native wages and go toward with the plan. In 1896 these trees yielded over six hundred pounds of coffee per acre and obtained 20 cents per pound in the London Market.

AFRICA FOR THE AFRICAN.

NATIVE CHRISTIAN'S HOUSE.

The natives quickly abandon the old one-roomed hut and build three roomed square houses as shown above gradually fitting them with tables, chairs, cup-boards, etc.

MITSIDI HOUSE.

This humble structure was first built on Zambesi Industrial Mission property. It was erected on the spot where it stands as a monument of a generous act on part of several Angoni men. It was on this wise: In or about the close of the year 1892 I reached this spot weary, sickly and weak. My little daughter was with me. A great tree stood where this house now stands. A drenching rain was falling. Several Angoni men were sheltering under a grass roof they had constructed on the boughs of that tree. They had made a fire there and were crouching round to keep warm during the cold rain for they had but little clothing. Yet these men out of their good nature got up instantly and insisted that myself and the little child should sit round that fire while they stood close around the trunk of the tree in the rain to get what shelter they could. They also offered us some of their corn which we roasted over

AFRICA FOR THE AFRICAN.

the fire. To me this and many other such instances prove the innate nobility of the Negro and speaks volumes as to his future greatness as a race.

Though the house itself is a clumsy first effort at building, yet the prospects from its veranda on the further side is as charming as the act just alluded to which caused the spot to be selected. It is thus described by a visitor:

We are now at Mitsidi House, still slightly troubled at the seemingly inaccurate reports of the wonderous scenery visible from this point. The house itself is built upon a ridge, flanked on either end by higher hills - one most appropriately named "Mount Prospect." We turn the end of the house towards the entrance, when lo! before our gaze bursts forth, in all splendour, a scene that might well be taken from fairyland - a scene that compensates in full all the toil in reaching it, and more than justifies the enlogiums bestowed upon it. No word picture can describe it, or brush depict it! One gazes upon it spell-bound. From one's feet the slope descends swiftly to the valley beneath, and a glorious panorama of hills and vales, streams and mountains, forests and plains, extends like a penciled map for eighty to one hundred miles! To the right rises the mighty weather-worn rocky brow of Michiru Mountains in imposing majestic grandeur - the silent guardian of the scene before us. To the left stands his counterpart, but of diminutive proportions in comparison. The air is so purely transparent that distances seems annihilated. The various objects of interest stand forth in clear and sharp relief, and the clouds, like mirrors, catch the ever varying changes of the sun's mood, partaking of his glory, as when his race is run, sinks into evening beauty.

Just beneath us, Ailsa Craig[179] stands out as if one might grasp it, a miniature ideal station, yet far enough away if computed by distance.

---

[179] **Named for an island off the coast of Scotland, Ailsa Craig is one of the colonial names which did not endure.**

Beyond, occupying the centre of the scene, rises a conical hill, which intervenes between Maliya and Mitsidi. Away again to the left, just peeping round the side of a towering hill, one can see a white patch in the dense green, which we are told is Chilingani Station. Beyond this again, hills succeed hill, engirdling the valleys, till they end in the boarders of the Shire Plains. Afar off, in Angoniland, they rise again, where range above range, they culminate in jagged uneven peaks of the Kirk Mountains[180], a fitting frame to a lovely picture.

A MISSIONARY CONVENTION.

---

[180] The Kirk Range extends along Malawi's border with Mozambique from Mwanza to Ntcheu.

Index

Aborigines' Protection Society, 22
Adventist Industrial Mission, Matabeleland, 35
African Christian Union, 26, 28, 66, 71, 72, 83, 92
African Development Society, 68, 72, 102
Afro-American, 41, 66, 68, 69, 90, 92, 102
Afro-American Christian Union, 66
Ajawa, 17, 50, 61, 84, 85, 87, 93
Albert Nyassa, 70
Amatongaland, 52, 53
America, 10, 14, 21, 28, 38, 39, 40, 44, 48, 54, 61, 65, 69, 80, 83, 87, 90, 92; See also United States
Angoni, 17, 86, 109
Angoniland, 111
Anti-Slavery Society, 22
Arabs, 11, 22
Atonga, 17
Australia, 73, 74, 77, 78, 79, 90
Bangevolo, 69
Baptist Church, 87
Baptist Industrial Mission of Scotland, 80
Baptist Missionary Society, 76n
Basutoland, 52, 53, 56
Bechuanaland, 52, 53, 55, 56
- Crown Colony, 53

Belgium, 19
Blantyre Mission, 77, 80, 82, 84-85n
Blyden, Dr, 32
Booth, Edward, 73, 77, 105
Booth, Emily, 77, 78, 109
British, 11, 17-21, 23, 27, 28, 38, 46, 47, 48, 50-53, 55, 56-58, 60, 62, 64, 69, 71, 84-88, 92
British Central Africa, 17, 23, 35, 69, 76
British Central African Protectorate, 20, 23, 47, 48, 86
British Imperial East Africa, 20, 48
British South African Chartered Company, 20, 57, 69
Caldwell, Robert, 79
Cape Colony, 52, 53, 83
Capetown, South Africa, 76
Carey, William, 76
Central Africa, 15-18, 20, 23, 30, 32, 45, 47, 57, 61, 79, 83-85, 93, 102
Cetewayo, 61
Chickunda, 17
Chilembwe, John, 61, 87, 93
Chilingani Station, 111
Chinde, 50
Chindi, 102
Chipalamaba, 50
Chipeta, 17, 93
Christian Settlement Proposal, 31

Church Missionary Society, 76n
Church of Scotland, 77, 82
Cocoa, 91, 94, 100
Coffee, 47, 71, 91, 94, 100, 105, 106
Colenso, Bishop John William, 60
Colonies, 27
Colony, 52, 53
Congo River, 45
Cotton, 71, 72, 100
Dickie, Alexander, 93
Dinizulu, 61
Douglass, Frederick, 32, 33, 43-45, 54
Durban, South Africa, 58, 59
Dutch, 11, 46, 52, 54, 62, 64, 83
East Africa, 20, 45, 48, 52, 57
East Central Africa, 30, 45, 93, 102
East London, South Africa, 58, 77
Emancipation, 22, 53, 88
England, 61, 75, 80
Europe, 10, 69
Fort Johnston, 86
Fort Liwonde, 86
Fort Sharp, 86
German East Africa, 52n
German West Africa, 52
Gomani, Chief 86
Henchman, Humphrey, 78
Hindu, 58
India, 21, 59, 76
Industrial Missions, 81, See also Adventists' Industrial Mission, Baptist Industrial Mission of Scotland, Nyassa Industrial Mission, Zambezi Industrial Mission
Jackson, Andrew, 12n
Jendo, 83
Johannesburg, South Africa, 55, 62
Johnston, Sir H.H., 17, 23, 57, 79, 86
Kahma, Chief, 55
Kapeni, Chief, 84, 85, 86
Kawinga, Chief, 85
Kimberly, South Africa, 62
King, Vice Consul, 50
Kirk Mountains, 111
Kumsumala, 50
Lake Nyasa, 50
Liberia, 32
Lincoln, Abraham, 89
Livingstone, David, 46, 76, 77, 84, 85
Liwonde, Chief, 85n, 86n
London, England, 18, 46, 48, 55, 58, 60, 64, 76, 77, 79, 85, 97, 107
Lovedale, South Africa, 82
Mackay, Alexander, 32, 76
MacRay, 76, See Mackay
Maize, 69, 72
Makalaka, 56
Makololo, 17
Malinka, Morrison, 93
Maliya, 111
Manganja, 17
Mangin, Edward, 77
Mashona, 56, 63, 64
Matabele, 56, 63, 64
Matabeleland, 35

M'Kanda, 85
Melbourne, Australia, 74, 77
Michiru, 110
Missionaries, 79, 81, 84-86
Mitsidi, 105, 107, 110, 111
Mount Prospect, 110
Mponda, 50
My Bondage and My Freedom, 32
Natal, 52, 53, 55, 60, 62, 84, 97
Natal Advertiser, 62
Niger Coast Protectorate, 20
North America. 10
Nyassa, 35, 50, 69, 79-81
Nyassa Industrial Mission, 35, 79, 80, 81
Orange Free State, 53-54
Pietermaritzburg, Natal, 84
Port Elizabeth, South Africa, 58
Port Herald, 50
Portugal, 19
Portuguese, 11, 48, 50, 52, 53, 85
Portuguese East Africa, 52
Rhodesia, 57
River Transport Service, 71, 102
Royal Niger Company, 20-21, 57, 69
Scotland, 77, 80, 82, 110
Scott, Rev. D.C., 82n, 84n
Scott, Dred, 12n-13n
Shire Highlands, 76
Shire Plains, 111
Shire River, 50

Slavery, 11, 13n, 17, 18, 21, 22, 27, 32n, 40, 46n, 50, 53, 85n, 86, 88, 89, 92
Sobantu, 60
South Africa, 15, 19, 20, 23, 45, 48, 52-55, 57, 58, 65, 69, 82, 83, 87, 97
South African Company, 19, 20, 52, 55
Spanish, 11
St. Helena, Island of, 61
Steamers, 102
Sugar, 47, 71, 72, 91, 100
Symes, Joseph, 74
Taney, Judge Robert, 12, 13
Tabnganyika, 69
Taxes, 14, 18, 23, 24, 36, 48, 49, 53, 57-60, 85, 87
Tea, 91, 94, 100
Tete, Mozambique, 102
Transvaal, 52, 53, 54
Uganda, 32, 76
United States, 9, 13, 33, 88, 92, 93, See also America
Victoria, Queen, 20, 22, 70
Virginia, USA, 42, 48, 87
Washington, DC, 32, 42
West Africa, 21, 52, 53, 57, 66
West Indies, 21, 32, 38, 39, 88, 90
Zambes(z)i Industrial Mission, 35, 79, 80n, 81n, 93n, 109
Zambesi River, 50, 63
Zomba, 18, 85
Zulu, 23, 46, 60-65, 83
Zululand, 52-53

www.ingramcontent.com/pod-product-compliance
Lightning Source LLC
Chambersburg PA
CBHW021834300426
44114CB00009BA/438